THE
WOMAN
FENCER

Nick and Anita Evangelista

Wish Publishing
Terre Haute, Indiana
www.wishpublishing.com

LCCN: 2001086541

Proofread by Ken Samelson and Heather Lowhorn
Cover designed by Phil Velikan
Cover Photo by Anita Evangelista
Interior Photos by Anita Evangelista, with the exception of those on pages iv, vi, 173, 175, 179, 185, 187 from the collection of Ralph Faulkner, on pages 12 and 15 from the collection of Polly Craus August, on pages 22 and 191 courtesy of Elaine Cheris, on page 182 courtesy of Mary Huddleston, page 194 courtesy of Roberta Brown, page 67 by Bob McEowen, on pages 8, 37, 44 and 54 by Nick Evangelista, and those on pages 41 and 47 by Justin Evangelista.

Printed in the United States of America
10 9 8 7 6 5 4 3 2 1

Published in the United States by
Wish Publishing
P.O. Box 10337
Terre Haute, IN 47801, USA
www.wishpublishing.com

Distributed in the United States by
Cardinal Publishers Group
7301 Georgetown Road, Suite 118
Indianapolis, Indiana 46268
www.cardinalpub.com

THIS BOOK IS FOR MY MOM

I'll go out there and fence any guy.

— Iris Zimmerman, United States Fencing Champion

PREFACE

I am not a woman, nor have I ever been one. But I have been in fencing for over 30 years, and have fenced with and taught hundreds of women. Young ones, medium-aged ones, and older ones. That, I believe, qualifies me for writing about fencing for women. Besides, I also know a little bit about the sport of fencing.

But, of course, no matter how much I know, I will never have a woman's unique perspective. That is why I have asked my wife, who is, in fact, a woman *and* a fencer *and* a registered nurse, to write the sections of this book that deal specifically with issues most relevant to a woman's needs as a fencer and an athlete.

I hope this book makes you — every woman — want to fence.

— Nick Evangelista

NOTE: Many of the candid photographs in this book are of beginning fencing students, and are not meant to be fully polished examples of form and technique.

TABLE OF CONTENTS

ACKNOWLEDGMENTS

Thanks first, as always, to my late, great fencing master, Ralph Faulkner.

Next, thanks to my wife Anita — writer, photographer, RN, EMT, and budding psychology student — for her major contributions to this book's content.

Thanks to my "adopted" aunt Polly Craus August for writing the foreword for this book.

Thanks to the multi-talented swordswoman and actress Roberta Brown for contributing the afterword for this book.

Thanks to my students Amanda Moore, Katy Emerson, Pat Drennen, Kat Jaklitsch, and Jamie Evangelista for posing for many of the photos appearing in this volume.

Thanks to all the women and girls who graciously shared their thoughts on fencing in the "Beginner" chapter of this book.

And, certainly thanks to the many women — students, friends, and acquaintances — who have contributed thoughts, ideas, and experiences that have become part of *The Woman Fencer*: Melinda McRae, Nanne Snow, Nora Cedar, Kellee Paterson, Kathleen King, Priscilla De Callier, Heidi Mayer, Pat Bedrosian, Ruth Botengan, Virginia Mekkelson, Marilynn Jordan, Marie Woolf, Jessica Smith, Rebecca Cisco, Lanie Frick, Sammie Smith, Halley Moore, Zoe True, Kat Jaklitsch, Judy Moore, Pam Mueller,

Judy Bowles, Melinda Henderson, Robin Douglas, Lilly Cross, Edie Ishii, Isabelle Pafford, Diana Viola, Sabina Martinez, Stephanie Strode, Marilyn Cook, Pat White, Liz Lachman, Wendy Wilkinson, Josie Rachford, Ronni Werner, Yasuko Nakajima, Sara Mason, Roberta Peart, Charlie Robinson, Amanda Moore, Pat Drennen, Katy Emerson, Sarah Niere, and Melodee Spevack to name a few among many.

Also, thanks to some guys: Jim Garrett, David Achilleus, Scott Stevens, Bill Gaugler, Rik Vig, Chris Amberger, Tom Cragg, Adam Crown, Bill and Patrick Shaw, Tom Greene, Peter Muhich, Bob Anderson, Lenard Voelker, Guy Bizek, Jeremy Beatty, Nigel Poulton, David Laloum, Neil Lazar, Kim Moser, John Blair Moore, Bill Leckie, Quinn Kellner, Warren and Wayman Coulter, Cliff Hadsell, Shaun Jackson, Philip Gentry, Bob O'Sullivan, Tim Weske, Bob Chapin, and, of course, Tony "Mysterious Circle" De Longis.

Finally, thanks to Holly Kondras for having faith in my wife and me to make this one of Wish Publishing's first titles.

Fencing Master and Author, Nick Evangelista

Polly Craus August

FOREWORD

A Fencer's Life

From the day I began fencing as a teenager in 1939, fencing has shaped my life. It has given me direction, friends, honors, and respect. During my fencing career, I was lucky enough to be a member of two Olympic fencing teams, first in 1948, and then again in 1952. I was also the U.S. Women's Individual Foil Champion in 1949. These were exciting times for me, experiences I wouldn't trade for anything.

My fencing master, the great Ralph Faulkner, was an Olympian in 1928 and 1932, the teacher of numerous champions, and one of Hollywood's great movie fencing coaches. From his expert training, I was led into an art and science as old as history. The Boss, as we called Mr. Faulkner, believed in me and gave me the opportunities to prove myself over and over again on the fencing strip. I gained a sense of myself, a belief in my own abilities. As a girl originally from a rural Texas background, a whole universe was opened up for me.

As a fencer, I was given gifts that have lasted a lifetime. I can truly say that even off the fencing strip, fencing shaped my world. I should mention here that I have dyslexia. Fencing, I know, gave me the focus and drive to overcome this handicap. Fencing also opened doors for me in my career as a script girl for a number of Hollywood movie studios. Industry people tended to take me more seriously as a champion fencer, even though the job itself had nothing to do with fencing. People saw me as a winner, as an accomplished athlete in a prestigious, somewhat exotic, field of endeavor, and so they were willing to put their faith in me. Even as a woman in a male dominated business, this was so. This gave me many more opportunities to use my judgment and creativity than I might have otherwise been allowed if I'd just been someone hired off the street.

Later, through my job, I met my future husband, Joe, who was a talented and successful movie studio cameraman. So, even my marriage, and resulting family, is connected in a direct line back to fencing. Moreover, today, years after I retired from competitive fencing, some of my best friends are still ladies I fenced with when I was a young woman. We have this bond, this tie that binds us together, despite the fact that all of us are separated by major distances on the map. We write, and we get together occasionally. Our fencing ties keep us connected to the world.

With every one of these things in mind, I can think of few other activities as compelling as fencing. So, have you thought of taking up fencing? I would recommend it. As both a physical and social exercise, it is excellent. It may not become the driving force in your life that it's been in mine, but, at the very least, it will offer you a unique challenge. Becoming a champion isn't everything. Sometimes just participating, achieving your own personal potential is enough. How good can you be? You won't know until you try.

Read *The Woman Fencer*, and find out what fencing is about and what it has to offer you.

— *Polly Craus August*

Polly Craus with her fencing master Ralph Faulkner, 1949.

Helene Mayer and Polly Craus

Be a fencer!

INTRODUCTION

A Fencing Book for Women

This is not a book about turning you into an Olympic fencing champion. It is not even a book that has organized competitive fencing as its goal. It is a book about teaching you to fence. Period! It is a book about developing a controlled, reliable foundation for an age-old art. What you do with that information is your own business. The outcome of your fencing will be the product of your goals, aspirations, abilities and determination.

Even more to the point, this is a book about teaching *women* to fence. Why women specifically? Wouldn't a nice, general fencing book do just as well? To one degree or another, you could say, yes, sure. Fencing is fencing, isn't it? Yes, fencing is fencing. But ... not necessarily. There are issues in life specific to women that can impinge on personal performance, issues that men do not experience. And since almost all fencing books are directed to a chiefly male audience, these unique aspects of womanhood have never really been explored in a fencing book. To my knowledge, there has never been a fencing book aimed only at women. From *Flos Duellatorum*, published in 1410, to my own *The Inner Game of Fencing*, published in 2000, this has been the case. Even fencing volumes penned by women fencers have not been gender exclusive in the direction of females.

There are books for women runners, women martial artists, and women interested in general health and exercise issues. Since more and more women are turning to fencing as a potential athletic pursuit these days, it is definitely time for women's fencing book.

While some of the information you encounter in this book will have a universal application in fencing, we've made a point to uncover and highlight material that has direct and significant application to women athletes. And, trust me, once you pick up that foil, épée, or sabre, you definitely become an athlete. Fencing is one of the most physically intensive sports you can engage in. It will be good to know about information that might affect your performance on the fencing strip or even your health. How you approach your training can impact your body and mind as much as the fencing itself. We will underscore balance in everything. Going overboard, becoming obsessive/compulsive, taking performance enhancing drugs, even in the name of success, is not a good thing. This is not a *win at any cost* book.

Fencing is a singular activity, requiring both mental clarity and physical adeptness. Knowing how to maximize your performance, whether it ends up being for nothing more than that evening of fun at the local salle or for the championship of the world, will only increase your chances for personal satisfaction. We want you to be the best you can be. We also want you to enjoy fencing for its own sake.

Now, go out there and take that first fencing lesson! Become a fencer!

SECTION ONE
HISTORIES

FENCING HISTORY

Men Without Women

Simply put, the history of fencing is largely a history bereft of women.

This is a fact.

Regretable and unfair.

But a fact, nevertheless.

Over the centuries women have, of course, been the object of more than one sword fight. But women have not been the movers and shapers of fencing thought and practice. The great masters — the Marozzos, the Cappo Ferros, the Angelos — were all very much of the male persuasion. The noted fencing books throughout the centuries have all been written by men. It was not until the latter part of the nineteenth century that women were even allowed, as a group, into the rarified world of fencing.

Origins

We can find evidence of organized sword-handling techniques among the ancient Egyptians, Babylonians, Greeks, and Romans. These forms, however, have had no impact on modern sword combat thought, and so remain footnotes to our story.

Actually, the Romans were quite systematic in their approach to sword fighting. Perhaps of all the ancient peoples of Europe, they were the most organized with regard to sword fighting. They had established schools of combat, qualified teachers, and an orderly process of technical training. Unfortunately, with the fall of the Roman Empire in the fifth century, all this organization was lost to the world.

We can look to the Middle Ages for evidence of sword combat struggling to regain some sense of order. Fencing schools flourished during this time, although it is doubtful that they were much more than congregating points for society's worst elements, predators who learned the martial arts for the sole purpose of preying on those weaker than themselves. Many towns banned fencing schools altogether because of the villainies associated with them. Fencing masters were lumped in with such unwholesome wretches as rogues, vagabonds, and ...actors! Obviously desperate characters. While some learning doubtlessly took place in such dark dens of iniquity, the teaching was by and large the product of individual preferences and fancies rather than scientific inquiry. In his book *The Art and History of Personal Combat* (1972), fencing historian Arthur Wise noted that the state of the fencing world of this time "did not encourage lively, analytical and discriminating minds into the profession."

Knights and Armor

The introduction of firearms into warfare during the late Middle Ages proved to be a compelling ingredient in the development of sword fighting.

Until this time, armor was a major factor in how sword combat was waged, at least among the upper classes, the knights and nobles. The common folk, as it has been noted, pretty much did what they pleased when it came to armed encounters. Armor provided the elite swordsman with all the protection he needed. It was his personal, mobile fortress. Because of this, the sword could be directed almost entirely to offensive maneuvering. In a way, because of this defensive dependence on armor, the growth of scientific sword handling was stifled.

Sword fighting during the Middle Ages (The Bayeau Tapestry)

But, with the invention of firearms, something interesting happened. Musket balls pierced armor, making it abruptly obsolete on the battlefield. Armor's thickness was increased to ward off the metal projectiles, but this only increased its ineffectiveness. It just became too ponderous to use.

In desperation, knights climbed out of their armor. But now, sans armor, they needed some way of protecting themselves. Sword-handling skills became the obvious method.

The upper class went to the lower strata of society for its instruction, as this was where non-armored swordsmen plied their trade. This infusion of the wealthy into the equation brought about radical change in the fencing scene.

It encouraged men to start thinking scientifically about combat. No longer was aggression and brute strength enough. The nobles and knights wanted more for their money.

Renaissance

Men of intellect began pursuing the study of sword fighting for both glory and the cash. Fencing was now an elite pursuit.

For a time, the early rough-and-tumble forms of swordplay held sway. They included punching, kicking, tripping, tumbling, and wrestling. Eventually, though, more and more attention was placed on what was going on with the swords alone.

Organization

The Germans brought organization to the fencing world. They organized guilds that held sway over sword combat in their homeland, the earliest of which was Fraternity of St. Mark. The Marxbruder, as they were known, ruled with an iron fist, and no one was allowed to teach without their permission.

Eventually, other groups were formed. Flourishing in an atmosphere of inquiry, they eventually overwhelmed Marxbruder authority. But the stage was now set for standardized thinking. Other countries, in time, established their own sword guilds.

Scholarship

The earliest written fencing studies began appearing around 1400, but the first fencing book of any real lasting importance, Achille Marozzo's *Opera Nova*, didn't see the light of day until 1536 (see illustration). Marozzo set down an approach to sword fightng that was more than tricks and rambling philosophical musings. By modern stan-

Marozzo's Swordplay

dards it may have been primitive, but, in his book *Schools and Masters of Fence* (1885), historian Egerton Castle notes that Marozzo's system was well in advance of any other at that period. It was truly a *system*. That *Opera Nova* was reprinted again and again for the next hundred years is a testimony to its value to the fencing world.

Other men joined in the quest for fencing excellence, each simplifying or complicating the sword fight according to his views and experience. Camillo Agrippa produced an uncomplicated form based on his own mathematical studies. Giacomo di Grassi advocated the thrust over the cut. Ridolfo Capo Ferro fixed the lunge as the primary method of delivering an attack. All these elements further produced a fencing form that was both logical and efficient, which made it easily reproducible.

The art and science of fencing was underway.

Cut or Thrust?

The late sixteenth century brought the invention of the rapier to fencing. The rapier was a point weapon, simply put, a thrusting sword. Suddenly, sword fighting technique took a new direction. No longer was the main emphasis of sword combat placed on the cutting edge of a blade but on its tip.

This innovation did not come without complaint, however. The old school of sword combat, the masters of the cutting sword, looked upon the rapier as a vile interloper. Not only did they see it as an imperfect, ineffective weapon, but also as a threat to their art and their livelihood. Late sixteenth century English fencing master George Silver remarked of rapier fencers in his book *The Paradoxes of Defense* (1599), "Bring me a Fencer, I will bring him out of his fence tricks with good downe right blowes."

For the time period, such an opinion may have had some validity. The cutting sword was a long established weapon, with a clear-cut approach to combat, while the rapier was still in its developmental infancy. The controversy over which form was better — the cut or the thrust — waged on for decades in the fencing world, leading to more than a few armed encounters when one school of thought happened to find itself in the company of the other. This, of course, was how differences of opinion were settled in those days.

The Point Triumphs

In time, the rapier proved to be a more efficient weapon than the cutting sword for personal combat. Through practical application, it became apparent that poking holes in an adversary was more damaging than haching on them. Not only did the rapier provide more lethal wounds, but rapier hits were more easily delivered.

By the end of the first quarter of the seventeenth century, the rapier had become the queen of swords.

Early rapier practice

Rapiers, Rapiers, Rapiers

Throughout the seventeen century, the rapier was being redesigned to be a more potent weapon. The blade was shortened, the weight lessened. The hand guard was redesigned over and over again to provide more protection for the sword hand. Fighting styles changed, too, to produce actions that reflected a more precise form of combat.

More and more, sword fighting began to resemble fencing as we know it today.

Italian Versus French

At this same time, fencing split into two distinct forms: the Italian school and the French school. The Italian school was characterized by a robust, physical approach to sword combat. The French school was distinctly academic, very much a mind-driven pursuit. As it turned out, the French method, because it was the more uniform of the two, proved the most easily taught. Because of this, the French school became the dominant style to fencing throughout Europe.

However, the French-Italian fencing rivalry exists to this very day.

Smaller is Better

In the development of the sword, the rapier gave way to the small sword, the dueling sword of the eighteenth century. The small sword was a cut-down, streamlined version of its predecessor. Light and easily maneuverable, it produced a style of fighting that was both highly mobile and very quick. Small sword combat became the epitome of sword fighting technique. It was precise, conservative, and balanced. Sword fighting theory never produced a more finished form.

The Turning Point

During the mid-eighteenth century, at the height of fencing's development, a strange thing happened: the

Swordplay in the seventeenth century

sword stopped being Europe's weapon of choice. The pistol had become sufficiently accurate by this time to appeal to a world now enamored of burgeoning technological advances. Whether in industry or the art of dispatching enemies this was so. The pistol took less physical skill to operate, and an opponent could be killed from a relatively impersonal distance. Even the most inept human being could aim and shoot a firearm. Almost overnight, the sword disappeared from the everyday operation of humanity's affairs.

The Sport of Fencing

Here, fencing took a new direction: sport. The art took precedence over the martial art. It was observed that fencing could be employed to improve health, poise, grace, and as a non-lethal competitive activity. The leading exponent of this notion was Domenico Angelo, a French-trained Italian master, who eventually set up shop in London. Angelo's salle became a focal point for society's elite, and he personally went on to teach members of England's royal family. Moreover, his book, *The School of Fencing*, set the stand for fencing technique for years.

Angelo taught fencing well into his eighties, and founded a fencing master dynasty that spanned a century and a half.

At this same time, we also see the foil, the practice weapon of fencing, being developed into a safe, flexible tool fit for recreational purposes. Fencing could now be approached for its own sake.

Modern Fencing

From here on, fencing developed quickly into the cast we are familiar with today. The fencing at the end of the eighteenth century — the form, the attacks, the parries, the nomenclature — is similar to that used by today's fencer. The nineteenth century brought the regular use of protective masks, the standardizing of fencing clothing, and formalized rules; also, women (finally!) began to take an active role in the sport. The twentieth century introduced competitive fencing on a worldwide basis, electric fencing weapons, greater opportunities for women fencers, and, in the less than grand tradition of modern sport, a growing obsession with winning at any cost.

Fencing at the start of the twentieth century

It is a fact, though, that fencing is growing more popular every year. *The United States Fencing Association*, the guiding body for U.S. fencing, reports that it's membership has never been healthier.

What will the future bring for fencing? Even as the less appealing aspects of fencing flourish, there is already a growing backlash against the aforementioned limited sport mentality. Many fencers, finding the modern approach shallow and pointless, have returned to a more classically-oriented game, emphasizing art and science in their quest for excellence. In response to this, sport fencers look on with amused disinterest. As in days of old, two warring mind-sets clash noisily. The more things change, the more they remain the same.

Will sport fencing continue with its present momentum, or will classical fencing overtake its more prosaic relative? Or will fencing take an altogether unanticipated direction brought on by presently unknown forces? Only time will tell. Fencing has always been, and always will be, a volatile entity, an almost living form. That's what makes it interesting.

A swordswoman insists on her rights

AMAZONS, ACTRESSES, AND ATHLETES

Women and the Sword

In spite of the fact that men have basically controlled the methods by which swords have been employed throughout the centuries, we can look back through legend and history to find distinctive instances of women being linked actively with swords. Whenever we come across such a moment, the women involved seem to have proven themselves more than worthy adversaries.

The Very, Very Olden Days

When we look for early accounts of women with swords, the Amazons of Greek mythology come to mind, warrior women who menaced the likes of such redoubtable heroes as Hercules and Theseus. Then, there were the fierce Celtic warrior women from Roman times, half-naked, sword-wielding females who fought side by side with their men. This was scary enough stuff for Roman soldiers to write home about it. And who can forget the occasional lady pirate, such as the infamous Anne Bonney, of whom it was said ended a number of love affairs with her trusty cutlass?

Much of this might be considered fanciful, or at the very least, exaggerated. But in legend there is often some degree of truth.

Women Swashbucklers

In our quest for historical women/sword connections, we might also consider the occasional female adventurer in the guise of a noblewoman or actress, who likewise happened to be a fencer/duelist.

In the sixteenth century, the Princess of Eboli, a great and wealthy lady of Spain, is chiefly remembered for an infamous murder in which she was implicated. But she is also remembered for having lost an eye fencing with a servant when she was still a girl. It should be understood that fencing masks had yet to be invented in the 1500s, and it took considerable personal fortitude to engage in any kind of sword practice.

Julie Maupin, a performer in the Paris Opera during the seventeenth century, is another noteworthy example of a notorious female personality engaged in fencing. The mistress of the great fencing master Serane, Maupin took many lessons from her lover in the art of the sword. She subsequently fought a number of duels. In fact she seemed to rather enjoy dueling. Perhaps her most infamous encounter followed a ball where, having offended a lady and being asked to leave, she announced that she would do so only if the gentlemen who confronted her would be so kind as to cross swords with her outside. Maupin led them outside, and slaughtered them one by one. (There is another ver-

Women pirates

sion of this story that has her fighting these duels masquerading as a man.) Although dueling was technically against the law — Louis XIV of France publicly condemned such private encounters and passed many strict edicts outlawing the practice — the actress avoided prosecution for murder. In point of fact, the king's outward displeasure was completely outweighed by his private admiration of duelists. Perhaps more so for a *woman* duelist. Anyway, Louis quickly pardoned Maupin. The actress later left France to became the mistress of the Elector of Bavaria. A hard-living woman, Julie Maupin died in 1707, at the *advanced* age of thirty-seven.

We can also look to the lives of the famous eighteenth century London-based fencing masters Domenico Angelo and his son Harry, both of whom taught many actresses the art of fencing.

Finally, with regard to historical accounts, there was the celebrated sword duel fought in Valduz, Liechtenstein, in August 1892, between the Countess Kilmannsegg and Princess Metternich, who quarreled over a particular flower arrangement at a recent art exhibition. Both women met stripped to the waist, swords in hand. Male servants were ordered to "avert their eyes." Fortunately, although both women were wounded after a few simple exchanges, the wounds were relatively slight. The duel was stopped without further bloodshed.

These, of course, are only brief moments from the pages of time. For a more concentrated look at women and fencing, we must move forward in time to the nineteenth century, when fencing had definitely become more sport than martial art.

The Sport of Fencing and Women

It is toward the end of the 1800s that we begin to witness an increasing number of women becoming enamored of fencing. This may have been due to the growing emancipation of women in modern society and an availability of leisure time due to the expanding industrial revolution. All over the western world, we suddenly see the ascendance of women fencers.

In the beginning, fencing for women may have been stressed primarily for recreational and health reasons, as competitive urges in women were not considered especially *ladylike*. But the opening was made, and women filled it enthusiastically.

In England, the French master Baptiste Bertrand and his son Felix were among the first masters to encourage women in general to fence. Originally, it may have been the realization that here was a completely untapped financial resource to be exploited, but even if this is true, the situation quickly translated into athletic/competitive terms. The Bertrands were rewarded with numerous individual female champions and many championship teams.

Restrictive Thinking

One of the earliest fencing clubs devoted entirely to women was the *London Ladies Fencers Club*, which was founded in 1901. But it was met with some skepticism.

The Duchess of Queensbury receiving fencing instruction in the eighteenth century.

Captain Alfred Hutton, one of the main exponents of fencing at that time, believed that fencing for women was just a fad, that women lacked the patience and follow-through necessary to produce successful fencers. As well-versed in fencing as he was, he was wrong.

In later years, fencing master Aldo Nadi emphasized that women should engage in fencing to keep their figures trim, to gain poise, and to tone the breast muscles(!). Perhaps not bad goals in themselves, but since these are pretty much his only comments on fencing for women in his book *On Fencing*, some modern commentators have suggested sexism in Nadi's tone. However, the Italian master was perhaps voicing a common theme for his time, especially among European males. To be fair, it should be noted that Nadi produced a number of capable female champions.

Certainly, at the outset of sport fencing for women, the limitations imposed by the establishment were obvious. Women were allowed to fence only foil. This was doubtlessly due to the fact that it was thought by the powers-that-be that épée and sabre were too strenuous, brutal, or dangerous for women. This practice continued for many decades into the twentieth century, but has since been dropped.

International Women

Although men had been competing in international events for decades, women competed in a world championship event for the first time in 1929. This competition was won by the great German fencer Helene Mayer. The first world champion team event for women took place in 1932 and was won by the women's team from Denmark.

Women fenced in a world championship épée tournament, both individually and as teams, for the first time in 1989.

On an Olympic level, women fencers were allowed to compete individually for the first time at the Paris Olym-

Women's fencing in the United States circa 1920.

pics in 1924. The Dutch fencer Ellen Osiier was the first women's Olympic foil champion. Women were given the opportunity to fence on teams at the Olympics for the first time at the Rome Olympics in 1960. However, they still only fenced foil. This event was won by the team from the Soviet Union. Olympic women competed in épée for the first time in 1996.

Competitive Results

On an international level, women fencers have very much paralleled their male counterparts with regard to the production of champion fencers. As with the men, Italian, French, German, and Hungarian women have traditionally ranked at the top of the list. Soviet women fencers came into their own in the 1960s.

Women's Fencing in the United States

In the United States, fencing for women progressed by degrees, closely following international trends, with the same kinds of barriers found in Europe. For one thing, women were simply slow to be recognized as legitimate athletes. While U.S. men had their first national tournament in 1892, U.S. women did not get theirs until 1912.

The first U.S. women's fencing champion was Adelaide Baylis.

Other constrictions placed on U.S. women fencers included four touch bouts, rather than five as they men had. Their foils were also of a slightly shorter length than those used by men. Since there are no logical reasons for such limitations beyond outmoded stereotypical mindsets, these two features of women's fencing are wisely no longer observed. Women fencers were also required to wear skirts until the 1930s. Lengths, of course, changed with styles and propriety. Now, all women fencers wear knickers.

Amazingly, after nearly a century of fencing in the U.S., women did not get their first national épée tournament until 1989. It was won by Susan Badders. Women's national sabre competitions did not begin until 1998. The premiere contest in this weapon was won by Kelly Williams.

On a college level, the Intercollegiate Women's Fencing Association was founded in 1929 to give women a greater voice in college fencing. One of its co-founders was fencing champion and coach Julia Jones Pugliese, who became the first woman coach of a U.S. Olympic fencing squad.

Now, women are fully represented in all aspects of fencing.

Present and Future of Women in Fencing

Today, although men and women do not compete together in major fencing competitions, there is relatively little that separates them on the fencing strip. Women receive the same type of training and are   expected to handle themselves with the same self-discipline as men. There is no coddling or silly overly-protective rules. After years of women's liberation looming over society's shoulder, very few hints that women fencers are somehow inferior to their male counterparts remain (a disparity in trophy size has been remarked upon in resent years, but that too will doubtlessly be rectified before long). In the record book, a woman's championship victory is deemed as meaningful and valid as any man's. And, of course, this is as it should be. Women have truly come a long way in fencing.

Where will fencing lead women in the future? Will all restrictions eventually melt away, with women competing officially with men in competitions at every level? Will men agree to this? Will women, as a group, even want this? Only time will tell.

Modern women fencers

U.S. CHAMPION WOMEN FENCERS

The following is a list of women who have been U.S. national fencing champions:

Foil

1912 Adelaide Baylis
1913 Mrs. William Dewar
1914 Margaret Stimson
1915 Jessie Pyle
1916 Alice Voorhees
1917 Florence Walton
1918 no contest (war)
1919 no contest for women
1920 Adeline Gehrig
1921 Adeline Gehrig
1922 Adeline Gehrig
1923 Adeline Gehrig
1924 Irma Hopper
1925 Florence Schoonmaker
1926 Florence Schoonmaker
1927 Stephanie Stern
1928 Marion Lloyd
1929 Florence Schoonmaker
1930 Elizabeth Van Buskirk
1931 Marion Lloyd
1932 Dorothy Locke
1933 Dorothy Locke

1934 Helene Mayer
1935 Helene Mayer
1936 Joanna De Tuscan
1937 Helene Mayer
1938 Helene Mayer
1939 Helene Mayer
1940 Helena Mroczkowska (Dow)
1941 Helene Mayer
1942 Helene Mayer
1943 Helena Mroczkowska (Dow)
1944 Madeline Dalton
1945 Maria Cerra
1946 Helene Mayer
1947 Helena Mroczkowska Dow
1948 Helena Mroczkowska Dow
1949 Polly Craus
1950 Janice York (Romary)
1951 Janice York (Romary)
1952 Maxine Mitchell
1953 Paula Sweeney
1954 Maxine Mitchell
1955 Maxine Mitchell
1956 Janice York Romary
1957 Janice York Romary
1958 Maxine Mitchell
1959 Pilar Roldan
1960 Janice York Romary
1961 Janice York Romary
1962 E. Takeuchi
1963 Harriet King
1964 Janice York Romary
1965 Janice York Romary
1966 Janice York Romary
1967 Harriet King
1968 Janice York Romary
1969 Ruth White
1970 Harriet King

1971 Harriet King
1972 Ruth White
1973 Tatyana Adamovitch
1974 Gay Jacobson (D'Asaro)
1975 Nikki Tomlinson (Franke)
1976 Ann O'Donnell
1977 Sheila Armstrong
1978 Gay Jacobson D'Asaro
1979 Jana Angelakis
1980 Nikki Tomlinson Franke
1981 Jana Angelakis
1982 Jana Angelakis
1983 Debra Waples
1984 Vincent Bradford
1985 Molly Sullivan
1986 Caitlin Bilodeaux
1987 Caitlin Bilodeaux
1988 Sharon Monplaisir
1989 Caitlin Bilodeaux
1990 Jennifer Yu
1991 Mary Jane O'Neill
1992 Caitlin Bilodeaux
1993 Felicia Zimmerman
1994 Ann Marsh
1995 Ann Marsh
1996 Felicia Zimmerman
1997 Iris Zimmerman
1998 Erin Smart
1999 Felicia Zimmerman
2000 Felicia Zimmerman

Épée

1981 Susan Badders
1982 Vincent Bradford
1983 Vincent Bradford
1984 Vincent Bradford
1985 Cathy McClellan

1986 Vincent Bradford
1987 Donna Stone
1988 Xandy Brown
1989 Cathy McClellan
1990 Donna Stone
1991 Margo Miller
1992 Barbara Turpin
1993 Leslie Marx
1994 Donna Stone
1995 Terry Lewis
1996 Leslie Marx
1997 Jessica Burke
1998 Arlene Stevens
1999 Arlene Stevens
2000 Stephanie Eim

Sabre

1998 Kelly Williams
1999 Nicole Mustilli
2000 Christina Crane

SECTION TWO
THE WOMAN
FENCER

The woman fencer

WHAT IS FENCING?

So, What is this Thing Called Fencing?

Fencing is the art and science of sword fighting. It is the ability to deliver a sword hit in either a sport encounter or a duel against one's opponent without being hit one's self. This last portion of fencing's description is very important because the ability or inability to recognize this reality defines a mindset that approaches fencing either as a precise, structured process or merely a game of counting wins and losses. Ultimately, the path you choose will determine what you end up getting out of fencing. If you possess patience, self-discipline, and a desire for personal growth, you will more than likely go for the former. If you are oriented toward the aggressive, ego-driven pursuit of victory, you will probably opt for the latter approach.

But think of this: fencing is so much more than merely covering the distance from point A (your blade tip) to point B (your opponent's chest). Fencing is about control, as opposed having things happen to you. It is about knowing, as opposed to guessing. It is about making choices, as opposed to just reacting. It is about interacting efficiently and effectively with another person, not brute force.

Fencing is a fascinating, multi-layered activity that brings into play knowledge of physics, psychology, and philosophy. It also requires a development of technical

Fencing!

proficiency, strategy, and physical grace. It is rich in history and tradition. And, if approached with a desire to learn, it will always remain fresh and alive for you.

Ideally, fencing can be like painting a picture. Each opponent you meet is a new canvas upon which to create a work of art. Every fencer has his or her differences, each necessitating altering your game to take into account these variations. This means you fence a little differently against every individual you meet on the fencing strip. To be able to accomplish this on a regular basis is one of fencing's biggest challenges and most satisfying pursuits. If you take the time to understand the whys and wherefores of fencing, you will become the sort of fencer that values the latter.

Remember, fencing can be nothing more than a shallow time-filler, or it can provide great personal insight. A touch can be just a touch, or it can be an expression of excellence. Experiencing one's personal best, I believe, is what fencing is truly about.

WHY FENCE?

Although once the prerogative of men and dominated by solely male thinking, fencing has become, in a way, a sexless sport, where personal ability and determination outweigh gender considerations.

Still, knowing the above fact, why would you personally, as a woman, want to take up fencing? No one fights with swords for real anymore. You're a full-time mom, a secretary, a high school or college student, a business executive. What, then, does fencing have to offer that should entice you into picking up a foil, sabre, or épée? Honestly speaking, fencing has a lot to offer. Such as...

Your Body

Let's start with the obvious: fencing is great exercise. Everyone needs exercise to be healthy. Fencing is a physically demanding activity that develops endurance, flexibility, and grace. Personal strength is improved, too, although strength should not be an overriding concern in fencing.

Your Brain

So, we have a plus for the body. But, ideally, the brain is also stimulated by fencing, probably more so than in any other sport. Fencing is very logical and practical, which promotes clear thinking. Problem-solving skills and judgment improve. How does this happen? Simply put, fencing is very much a strategy-driven endeavor. With every action we produce, we encounter the concept of cause and effect. You do *this*, your opponent does *that*, you do *this*. We might call fencing a game of *physi-*

Fencing stimulates the mind and the body

cal chess. Engaging the brain constantly, generating ideas and testing them, really does stimulate the thought process.

Skill

As the mind focuses, directing and redirecting action, it starts to blend smoothly into the physical game, until mind and body become one efficient whole. Now, this *mind/body* factor of fencing has a neutralizing effect. By developing it fully, any woman can compete on an equal footing with even the most hulking male opponent. It is the successful inclusion of clear thinking in a stressful, physical situation that produces an effective use of body and blade that may be employed to negate strength and mindless aggression. Fencing is infused with techniques to overcome, to sidestep, the most brutal opponent you'll ever meet. Keep this in mind if you happen to be small and not so strong. Obviously, this fact is not gender exclusive. Both women and men can learn to exploit this feature of the game. Fencing is very democratic in this respect. Success goes to the skillful, rather than the brutal.

Age

The above truth even translates into an *age* factor. You have to give up some sports at the onset of middle age. Fencing is not one of them, however. A fencer can keep active well into old age. I have known women, and men, who fenced well into their seventies and still found it as satisfying as they did in their youth. My own fencing master was 95 years old when he died, and he taught right up until a few weeks before his death.

Variety

If you want a game with never-ending variety, fencing will fill that bill, too. The strong mental input sees to that. Strategic diversity keeps fencing from becoming static and predictable. Running or weightlifting or tennis or ping pong or hockey will not give you this. You can fence for 50 years, and it will always be different.

Self-Assurance

As a physical activity that deals with imposing oppositional behavior, fencing develops a strong sense of personal confidence (especially good for very young girls). Through self-discipline, it creates poise and balance.

Complexity

Fencing definitely has something for everyone. Besides the obvious sport element, we can find history, movies, psychology, physics, literature, and philosophy woven into its fibers. Fencing is anything but one-dimensional.

Competition

If you happen to be an aggressive, competitive female,

Social interaction in one fencing setting

fencing is geared to embrace this. Women are not looked down on for these qualities in fencing. Assertive behavior is an asset on the fencing strip.

Recreation

Your local fencing salle is a good place to relax and unwind and let the cares of the day take a backseat for a while. Meeting someone on the fencing strip, blade in hand, can become your only concern for two or three hours a couple times a week. Some of my students take lessons for this reason alone.

Social Interaction

Looking for social contact? Fencing is a very interactive pursuit. It's a good place to meet people. Sometimes the real challenge of fencing is keeping it from becoming *too* socially-oriented. You know, more talking than fencing. But fencers do date one another, that's a fact. I have mentioned this before, but I will say it again: I met my wife for the first time at the school where I taught in Hollywood. Moreover, today, most of my best friends are fencers or former fencers. Fencers form bonds that last.

The Money Factor

If you are an economically-oriented individual, fencing is a relatively inexpensive sport to get into, equipment-wise. Lesson costs tend to be on the conservative side, too. When compared to other sports, such as golf, skydiving, motorcycling, surfing, scuba diving, sailing, or tennis, where you can spend an arm and a leg purchasing really good equipment not to mention taking lessons, fencing looks pretty good.

Pleasure

Finally, fencing is just plain fun.

HOW TO GET STARTED IN FENCING

Making Decisions

In a way, the hardest part of learning to fence is just getting started. I can't tell you how many folks over the years have said to me, "Gee, I always wanted to learn to fence, but I just never did anything about it." That decision to really take the plunge — not just talk or fantasize about it — is a difficult one. It means deciding to confront reality. And sometimes that can be a frightening prospect. Will I like fencing? Will I do well? Will I get hurt? Will I look dumb in front of other people? These are all questions that run through the minds of prospective fencers. They ran through my brain 30 years ago. Other fencers have told me the same thing about their own introduction to fencing. There are personal demons to be confronted here, and certainly the easiest thing you'll ever do with regard to fencing will be to find excuses for not fencing. The best way to approach getting started is to just go out and do it. Don't think about all the possibilities of what you might encounter. Just leap in.

I can tell you one thing for sure, if you wait for the right moment to start taking fencing lessons, you will never begin. There is no right moment. There will always be things that get in the way. There will never be enough time in your life. You will always be pulled in 20 directions at once. That is the way life is. Make a decision.

The master and the beginner

Approach

Here is something that most beginners never think about: What approach do you want to take with regard to your fencing? That is, what do you want to get out of your fencing, and how serious are you? Fencing provides a number of avenues of expression. One that might be right for that person over there won't necessarily be the correct one for you. Let's take a look at what's out there:

Sport Fencing

The heavy emphasis here is on competition, organized competition, tournaments. That means being concerned with tournament results — winning and losing. Aggression, strength, and speed are often the hallmarks of the sport fencer. If you are of a combative nature and thrive on competition, sport fencing will appeal to you.

Classical Fencing

I have to admit that this is the form of fencing that is closest to my own heart. It was the method my own training took over 30 years ago. My master was a classical fencer, and his master before him was a classical fencer. That's three generations of classical thought that stretch back well over 100 years in an unbroken thread. The emphasis here is on mastering the art and science of fencing. Excellence in the sport part of the game is merely the byproduct of excellence in one's technique and strategy. Attention is paid to form, style, and self-discipline — the process of fencing, the inner game. Results are always viewed through this personal filter. I would say that this traditional route offers the greatest opportunity for personal growth.

Recreational Fencing

If you just want to have fun, this is the way to go. This form of fencing is as much a social event as it is sport. Recreational fencing can be a springboard to a more serious relationship with fencing, but be ready for a more casual setting overall.

Historical Fencing

Historical fencing is a relatively recent addition to the fencing world. By and large, the historical fencer rejects the concerns and precepts of modern fencing, and focuses instead on the use of historical weapons — such as the broadsword, the rapier, and the small sword — as they believe they would be employed in bygone centuries. There is often a sense expressed by those involved in historical fencing that they are learning a true martial art rather than a mere game. There may even be an arrogance expressed. My own thought is that historical fencing, if approached at all, should be an adjunct to modern fencing, as modern fencing provides a strong foundation upon which to build a historical understanding.

SCA Fencing

This type of sword fighting is a product of *The Society For Creative Anachronism* (SCA), a historically-oriented organization, with a strong emphasis on costumed role

A fencing school

playing, focusing especially on the Middle Ages. The SCA's combat is therefore inspired by earlier times, although it has been observed that it is perhaps more idiosyncratic than historically accurate. The SCA also places a strong emphasis on social interaction, with members taking on the persona of medieval nobles, knights, and ladies. The fantasy element of the SCA has made it an immensely popular organization with a huge membership worldwide. What can you say? It is what it is.

Theatrical Fencing

If you are an actor in need of fencing skills for a movie or a play, this form of fencing will be of the most use to you. Where the sport of fencing develops finesse and economy of movement, theatrical fencing exaggerates and dramatizes. Where the outcome of fencing is a satisfying conclusion for the participants, the goal of theatrical combat is to produce a pleasing effect for an audience. This should not, however, be looked on as a suggestion for actors to divorce themselves from actual fencing training. My own teacher, Ralph Faulkner, who worked with such swashbuckling luminaries as Errol

Flynn, Douglas Fairbanks, Jr., and Basil Rathbone during Hollywood's *golden age*, believed that actors should always have a thorough grounding in standard fencing methods before tackling theatrical material. This was done for two reasons, first, to hone physical skills, and, second, to promote a real understanding of one's actions. In this way, an actor might be more likely to produce sword encounters that would be both believable and safely executed. I have also found this to be true in my own theatrically-oriented teaching.

Schools and Clubs

Now that you have some idea of what you're looking for with regard to content, you need a place where you can actually learn to fence.

Schools and clubs can be located in a number of ways. The most immediate avenue to finding a place to fence is your phone book. Next, you might check with nearby colleges and universities, which often provide fencing in the form of teams, campus clubs, or courses offered to the community. This also goes for YMCAs, community centers, recreational and health clubs, and fraternal organizations. If these avenues fail, you might check for fencing schools with your local Chamber of Commerce; they usually know what's going on in the community. Of course, if you have access to a computer, the internet has a number of fencing-related sites that list schools across the United States. Finally, *The United States Fencing Association* (USFA), the guiding force behind competitive fencing in this country, may be able to help you find a school. (You can find a listing for the USFA in the back of this book.)

Schools of Thought

There are two official schools of fencing thought and technique: the French and the Italian. Both are unique and distinct, mirroring the mind-sets and personalities of the countries that developed them.

Beginning with foil

The French style of fencing is "academic;" that is, it is driven primarily by thought. This strategic approach is very pliable, giving way or avoiding rather than opposing directly. Adopting the French style, you never meet your opponent head-on. Rather you learn to sidestep everything he or she does, to turn their actions back against them. In my opinion (and I am prejudiced), it is the most applicable approach to a wide variety of physical types and abilities.

The Italian school is more physically oriented than the French, which makes it a decidedly confrontational or oppositional game. It is a distinctly "in-your-face" approach to fencing. A fencer trained in the Italian school likes to physically dominate his or her opponent on the fencing strip, overwhelming them. The Italian school provides a strong game for those who can master it.

There is also an unofficial school of fencing, a fairly modern creation, a kind of international, generic game. While it borrows bits and pieces from both the French and Italian schools, it is in fact an artificial construct, relying chiefly on pure athleticism to produce touches, which, in fact, is all it is meant to do. Tactics over technique. Results over process. More traditionally trained fencers consider it an undisciplined mess totally lacking in those qualities that have made fencing what it is for the last 500 years. But, to be honest, this new form is doubtlessly the most popular approach to fencing today. Why? Because it requires little or no mastery to engage in it — only muscle, speed, and aggressive intent, which gives those who follow this route "instant" fencing.

Equipment

Obviously, you'll need fencing equipment before you can start fencing. Some schools offer beginners the use of gear to get them started. But if you stay with fencing, you'll eventually want your own stuff. In fact, you'll never be more than a beginner if you don't eventually fork over the bucks for the trappings of fencing. Why is this? Well, for one thing, fencing is an intensely personal activity, which means you never get anywhere using gear that everybody else uses — you just don't develop a feeling for it. Second, without your own gear, you can never practice on your own, which you must do to be good. And, third, to become a fencer, you have to identify with fencing completely, and you can't make this leap without owning your own equipment. I have seen this to be the case for as long as I have taught fencing. You have to make a physical/financial commitment.

So, what equipment will you need?

Weapons are your starting point. Begin with a foil. The foil is the traditional teaching weapon of fencing. We'll talk more about this later.

After a weapon, buy yourself a fencing glove and get used to wearing it as quickly as you can, because you can't fence without one. If you ever get hit on the hand by an opposing blade — and you will — you will understand why this is the case. Furthermore, wearing a glove

Everything you need: jacket, gloves, mask, épée — note that this fencer is wearing normal sweat pants and tennis shoes

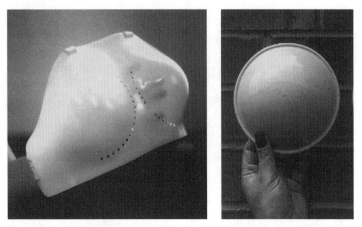

Breast protectors for women fencers

makes it easier to grip your foil.

Next, go for a fencing mask. I'd suggest a good three-weapon mask (one designed to accommodate foil, épée, and sabre), as they tend to be the sturdiest. I've used the same three-weapon mask for the past 20 years.

Then comes the fencing jacket, and, because you are a woman, breast protectors. Don't think you can get by without breast protectors, even if your jacket is padded. One hard touch to the chest without one will tell you why wearing them is a good idea.

Fencing pants, or knickers, are optional for casual fencing but are a requirement for competition.

Shoes? Any kind of athletic shoes will do. You can buy fencing shoes, but they are not vital to your situation. Just make sure what you have has good traction on the soles.

Finally, do yourself a favor and buy an equipment bag to carry all your gear in. It'll make your fencing life so much easier. You won't end up forgetting something important for your fencing class, and you won't keep spearing your friends and family and pets with your exposed foil blade. Besides, it's much easier to lug around an armload of unwieldy equipment in a bag with a shoulder strap on it than it is to juggle a lopsided pile in your arms. I've tried transporting gear with and without a bag. Believe me, *with* is definitely better.

Anyway, this is what you need to know to get started in fencing.

Now, go out there, and do it!

BEGINNERS' VOICES

Over the years, I have received numerous letters from women — young and old —who've decided to take up fencing. I'm always interested in their individual stories. I think the take of beginners is compelling because they have an untainted view of fencing. Their thoughts haven't had time to be overshadowed by peer pressure or ego. Their minds are the beginner's mind, fresh and waiting for the possibilities fencing has to offer.

I'd like to share with you a few novice thoughts that have been shared with me:

❈◈❈

"I fence because it is fun and really good exercise. There's no pressure to rush through training because you don't have to worry about being at the same level as anyone else. You learn at your own pace. I like fencing because it is so personal. You have to rely on yourself to get a good score, and not on a team to get points for you. I am 14 years old."   — A.M.

❈◈❈

"The only fencing I was exposed to as a child was what I saw in the movies, but even then I thought it was absolutely beautiful. I loved movies about knights, maidens, and swordplay. Although I'm just now learning to fence, I have a new appreciation for the duels I saw onscreen. I've found learning *about* fencing just as fascinating as learning *to* fence. I am intrigued by the history of fencing just as I find myself excited by the act of mastering form and point control. I enjoy listening to the stories and experiences of others as I am forming my own. It's interesting to see how other students have their own reactions and responses to the same things I'm learning. The physical side of fencing can be demanding, but I love watching my foil quiver under the fatigue of my inexperienced arm. I love it because with every lesson I take I come closer to my goal of becoming a fencer. I know that, having just begun fencing, I have a long road of lessons and learning ahead of me, and I look forward to experiencing what I see as both an exciting pastime and an art form."   — *S.D.N.*

✠◈✠

"What makes me want to fence? Well, lots of things. It makes me feel special and unique. It helps me stand out in a crowd, and in a good way. It makes me different from everyone else. Even better, when you are fencing, you get great exercise while having fun. In my opinion, I think fencers have more confidence in themselves than other athletes. Why? Well, you don't know what the other fencers are thinking, and you have to depend on yourself totally. In basketball, you could make a bad pass, and your teammates could give you a look that says, 'That was a dumb thing to do.' In fencing, you are less self-conscious, for one thing, because all fencers are wearing masks. You don't know what your opponents think of you, and they don't know what you think of them. Everyone's thoughts are kept mostly private, and I think this gives you more concentration and confidence while competing. I am 14 years old, so I have much more to learn about fencing. Through my lessons, I plan to learn much more about it, as well as how I can improve myself." — *K.E.*

✠◈✠

"My name is Roberta and I'm new to fencing. I'm 38 years old and a mother of two small children and three older stepchildren. Since I don't work outside the home, I felt I needed something to call my own. Fencing is it! I love it as much as I used to love riding my horse back when I had the time and money to do it. Many of the folks at the club where I fence give me lessons for free, and they are also nice. But my favorite teacher is Joe Pechinsky! He is in the fencing hall of fame. Joe always calls me over to him for a lesson. He tells me to come and see him right away so that he can make sure he will have time to teach me. He is 83 years young! I feel honored to be taught by him."

— *R.P.*

✠◈✠

"I have only just begun fencing, although it has been a dream of mine for a very long time. I wish to improve myself through continued study and application. I find that adding fencing to my life has opened up a whole new world, and I am pleased to be part of it. I am a person steeped in history and traditions ... as a sculptor I work to portray human form, and now I have a different way to approach my passions."

— *M.R.*

✠◈✠

"I was in my first tournament earlier this month. It was a dry tournament, so we didn't have to run out and buy electric. The idea was to go out and have some fun with it. I watched the best novice fencer in our group do some head trips on herself about her physical endurance, as well as she felt guilty about not being with her family that day. Despite our trying to refocus her, she came in third. Another young fencer, who sometimes has problems settling down, did great and came in first. We are very proud of her! I think because I didn't expect much (I am older than most of the fencers) and took each match on its own merit — and some dumb luck — I came in second!!! I was very tickled about it. (Like the returning Roman generals, I should have someone whispering in my ears, 'Thou art mortal.') I do know that I have a long way to go before I am really a fencer!"   — *M. J.*

"At 65, I was faced with retirement and a loss of my definition as a professional. It seemed a daunting perspective. It was time to look for an intellectual challenge that could also meet my need for physical conditioning. After a long search, fencing became my focus. It encompassed the physical workout my body required and the intellectual stimulation that keeps me engaged. My instructor has assured me that I can retain my efforts in fencing well into my elder years. Fencing incorporates discipline, physical effort, intellect and rewards with panache. The perfect answer to keeping the second half the best years of your life."

— *P.D.*

"I love fencing, but I do find it somewhat frustrating at times. I had been a figure skater and a ballet dancer for many years, and I thought, erroneously of course, that fencing would be a piece of cake. I thought I could just watch someone do it and copy them! Can you imagine that? I'm taking flamenco dancing also, and that's much easier for me than fencing. Still, I am determined to make a go of it. I really look forward to my lessons. Well, that is an understatement. I don't know what I'd do without them!"

— *P.D.C.*

FENCING FOR GIRLS

If it is approached right, I think fencing can be one of the most beneficial activities kids can engage in — especially for girls, who are often cast in stereotyped roles from a very early age. "Girls do this, girls don't do that." Individualistic in the extreme, fencing can teach a girl to think for herself, to be a person who makes self-confident choices instead of having the world just happen to her.

Official and Organized

There is a growing number of kids today getting into fencing, and quite a few of them happen to be girls. Since 1996, the number of registered fencers under the age of 20 in the *United States Fencing Association* (USFA) — fencing's governing body in the United States — has tripled, to over 9,000, and more than a third of this group is female.

The aforementioned USFA has a very strong youth movement, the Junior Olympic program, which was begun in 1972. To its credit, the J.O. caters equally to boys and girls. Besides holding local, regional and national tournaments, the USFA holds camps and clinics for young fencers. The goal is to produce future international champions.

Fencing is an ideal activity for young women

Competitive Girls

We can look back to the early part of the century to German fencer Helene Mayer, who won the championship of Germany in 1923 at the ripe old age of 13. At 17, she easily captured a gold medal at the 1928 Olympics in Amsterdam, Holland. She is considered by many to be one of the greatest fencers of all time.

More recently, U.S. fencer Iris Zimmerman became the first American in history to win a world championship event — the 1995 under-17 women's foil — at the age of 14. Her younger sister, Felicia, became the first female fencer in history to win three gold medals at a single Junior Olympics in 1991. She has also won more World Cup medals than any other American fencer, male or female, with five.

I highly recommend fencing for the younger set. On a mental level, it develops self-confidence, pride, judgment, and a sense of uniqueness. Physically, it stimulates balance, flexibility, and endurance. This makes fencing ideal for developing personalities and bodies. Fencing can be a springboard to a well-balanced life as an adult.

A Good Time to Start

A good time for girls to start fencing is between the ages of 10 and 14 (which is about the same for boys). This is a time when the capacity to concentrate strengthens. Also, coordination stabilizes dramatically.

Anything prior to this age period depends on the individual child. Girls do tend to be a bit more receptive to the intricasies of fencing at a slightly younger age than boys do. But this is true of many activities, not just fencing.

Pitfalls

Parents should be supportive of their kids and then get out of the way. Parents who force their kids into sport for the parents' glorification are a menace to their child's

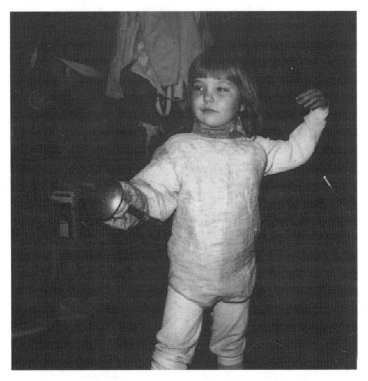

Fencing gives young girls a sense of confidence

learning process and to every sport they touch. They're sometimes called "little league" parents or "stage" parents. They push their kids; they get into fights with officials and other parents, they burn their kids out. Fencing should be enjoyable, not a chore or obligation.

Parents can also be overly protective, which tends to make the child self-conscious. Fencing has a rite of passage, and to become a real fencer, you take some lumps.

I've also had parents and children come to me for joint fencing lessons. The let's-do-something-together syndrome. Invariably, the parents stick with the lessons while the kids fade away into other activities. This is true especially if you have a wide disparity in ages such as adult 40, child 6. You can't talk to them on the same level at the same time. So, when you deal with the child, you ignore the adult. If you work with the adult, the kid becomes bored silly very quickly. It's even worse when the child outdoes the adult. I think the best approach for kid/parent fencing lessons is for them to have completely separate sessions and compare notes later on. Then, they develop their own fencing identities.

Fencing can be character building. This should be a major goal for parents. Winning is secondary. A child who sticks with fencing from an early age will become good, whether winning is stressed or not. If you accept this as fact from the start, the potential for harm will be minimized greatly. If the fencing process is allowed to move forward naturally, even ego-related problems tend not to materialize. We hope that you can find a teacher who will guide your daughter, or son, through the rocky traps that are inherent in fencing — or, let's face it, in any competitive activity.

In the end, if you do it right, fencing will mean something for your child beyond a mindless accumulation of points. It may even be something they continue with for their entire lives.

Teaching kids to fence

FENCING FOR THE MATURE WOMAN

More and more, the value of exercise for senior citizens is being underscored in our modern world — especially for older women, who face a number of health related challenges that men do not necessarily encounter. This includes such striking problems as loss of bone density through lack of exercise. It has been proven that even mild exercise can work wonders on the health of our more mature citizens, women and men. Fencing can easily provide such a workout. An older lady doesn't have to go out and mix it up on the fencing strip with the 20-year-olds. Even simple lessons may be enough to furnish a positive result.

The aforementioned bone enhancement is doubtlessly important in the area of hip problems, a known scourge for today's elderly. But we can also look to fencing to provide other benefits, such as weight reduction, improved blood circulation, a healthier heart, a stronger immune system, a better overall mood, an increase in deep sleep, and a heightened sense of personal accomplishment.

I'm not claiming that fencing is the only way for an older woman to get such exercise, only that it is a highly accessible and enjoyable way to do so. Fencing, however, does possess an ingredient many physical activities lack, that of really having to think — even in the limited confines of a lesson — which produces the added

The mature woman fencer

benefit of stimulating the mind. Now, you don't even have to be old for *that* to benefit you, but for the elderly such a plus may be the difference between a sparkling mind at 90 and the catastrophic mental deteriorations often associated with getting old.

Of course, any exercise should be undertaken in conjunction with a proper diet and a doctor's expert input.

Should you, a woman of mature years, take up fencing as a physical discipline? I have had a number of women students in their fifties and sixties, and one or two in their seventies, and, invariably, they all found fencing to be an enhancement to their lives. Will it be for you? Like I said, it isn't necessary to go for the gold medals or to even go for bouting with the kids. Try fencing because it's different, because it might be fun, because everyone needs exercise.

WOMEN VERSUS MEN

Everyone is equal when they walk onto the fencing strip. You come to every bout fresh, with neither advantage nor disadvantage in terms of artificial supports. You want to win; your opponent wants to win. You pit your skill against another fencer's skill, and that is that. It is up to you to prove your superiority through the application of your technical knowledge with every encounter. This is the only true yardstick of fencing. What you did yesterday or last week or last year doesn't matter. The time to fence well is *now*.

As men and women, we might think of ourselves as having advantages and disadvantages, but, in fencing, this is a very transitory concept. The acquisition of technique and strategy is there for anyone to master. Skill is the great equalizer. If you are down today, there is something in fencing for you to learn that will put you on top in the near future. Desire, perseverance, and patience are your ultimate keys to success. In this sense, it doesn't matter if you are a woman or a man. Fencing is not a gender-specific activity. *Your foil doesn't know if you are female or male.*

As a woman, over the course of your fencing career, you will doubtlessly fence against more men than women, only because there are always more men fencing than women. But this does not mean you are inferior on the fencing strip.

Foil fencers

Men certainly tend to be more physically oriented than women. We have the strength, the weight, the speed, and the aggressive tendencies that give us the edge in this area. But this is not necessarily what fencing is about — unless you decide to make it so. *Fencing is not about power*. In fact, focusing on the physical alone is the antithesis of good fencing. There are things to be learned in fencing that take you beyond the brick wall of strength.

For instance, let's talk about my specialty, the French school of fencing. Within the French school, we have techniques and strategies that sidestep the physical difficulties you may find facing you. We have blade evasions, non-resisting parries, and leverage-based offensive and defensive actions that easily defuse strength. Remember this: Your opponent may be twice as strong as you, but if he can't control your blade, if he can't touch you physically, then it is as though he has no strength at all. Aggressive actions that go nowhere, that produce no positive effect, mean nothing. It does take time to learn how to keep out of a brutal opponent's way, but it can be done. And it should be done. There is no excuse for using force against force. This is not what real fencing is about.

Women versus men

Another thing: since pistol grip weapons encourage both strength and heaviness in fencing, I would urge every woman reading this book to stay away from such devices as though they were the plague. You might find fencing an opponent armed with a pistol grip a bit daunting in the beginning — you may even be disarmed from time to time — but you will eventually learn how to deal with such ponderous nonsense. The finesse you gain from learning to fence with your fingers — as opposed to your entire sword arm — will last you a lifetime.

Don't opt for quick fixes or shortcuts in fencing. Rely on the gifts you possess. If you are small, you may also be light on your feet. Learn to use timing and distance to your advantage. Make yourself a difficult target to hit. Another goal should be developing finger dexterity rather than muscles. Forget completely the overpowering *smash-and-poke* approach. From my own experience, the latter is where a lot of male fencers end up, and it is a very limited game indeed.

As for speed, don't worry about being faster than other fencers. Timing and strategy are far more important. Speed only has value when it is delivered with the focused resolve and control that experience grants. If you get somewhere before your weapon point does, you might as well be the slowest turtle on the track. You're not going to hit anybody. Rather, be deliberate and base your actions on your opponent's behavior. Create holes in his or her defense by simply placing your blade where their blade isn't. This is fencing at its best.

SECTION THREE
WOMEN'S
ISSUES

Emotional, Psychological and Physical
by Anita L. Evangelista, BSN, RN, EMT

MIND AND HEART

The Emotional Side

No one comes to fencing as a blank slate, awaiting the sword's point to write some experience onto her life. Women who fence often bring a good deal of emotional baggage along to the first lessons — and some of that baggage is hard to set down. It helps to recognize that you're not alone in these concerns.

The Issues We Bring to the Strip

Like many youngsters of my generation, my first exposure to the sword was at Zorro's hand — not just any Zorro, mind you, but the REAL Zorro — actor Guy Williams in Walt Disney's version of the story. Decades later, I still can't watch any of the fine Zorro movies (including the latest version with actor Antonio Banderas), without thinking that these are IMPOSTORS not the real thing. I see Guy Williams's heroic smile — the bright light of those perfect teeth, that dashing and devilish charm — and I am transported to those fantastic duels, fighting the evil Commandante, bringing peace and freedom to "my" village, to "my" people.

Except, of course, that in my childhood fantasies, it wasn't Zorro who did these amazing deeds — it was me. I was the dashing swordswoman, leaping from rooftop to rooftop, my black silk cape swirling gracefully, my gleaming rapier making short work of the slobs and arrogant bullies who control my beloved pueblo. The entire community, naturally, just ADORED me.

Enter reality.

The Bad Guys don't carry single-shot muskets, don't fight on rooftops, and don't use swords. The hero isn't necessarily attractive, tall, or the possessor of a really nice smile. Silk garments tear easily and are hard to keep beautiful. Even if you do all the right stuff, some people will dislike you. You won't win all the time. Mostly, nobody else cares.

Important Issue Number One: Reality

Women first come to fencing with an inner image of their own physical prowess — that she will pick up a foil and immediately be great.

Life is not the same as the movies. Intellectually, we already know this — but that powerful inner mind keeps making comparisons: How come I'm not as thin as I should be? How come my fencing uniform gets those embarrassing stains under the arms? How come I lose more often than I win?

This is a hidden but very pervasive problem of our era — that many people have submerged their perception of reality beneath the constant barrage of images fed to us from birth by the entertainment industry. Because this is a subconscious influence, we don't challenge the images and assumptions they create — these ideas are left alone to underlie, confuse, and distort our perceptions of reality.

Competitive sports, such as fencing, are excellent "reality-induction agents." By taking up the foil, putting on the protective gear, and positioning yourself face-to-face with another fencer, you place yourself in a very real world where every action you take leads to a response from your opponent — and where actions you don't take result in touches against you. You begin to focus on the actual task at hand, and all the unnecessary daily worries, fears, doubts and confusions become minor — and may slip away entirely.

It helps to keep in mind that you will sweat, you will get very sore muscles, you will make embarrassing (to you) mistakes, at times you will feel like people are looking and laughing at your clumsiness (they won't be). These negative feelings WILL pass, and you WILL improve your skills with every lesson!

Important Issue Number Two: Competitiveness

Women, innately, tend to be peacemakers — settling disputes between our kids, finding a soothing word for quibbling colleagues at work and school, willing to accommodate ourselves to nearly any situation rather than "cause a problem." These are wonderful and necessary skills.

So strong is this innate characteristic in women generally, that one high level women fencer says, "I can't fence unless I'm really angry ..." In other words, she doesn't feel it is appropriate to "attack" or "compete" unless her inner restrictions are overridden by an adrenaline-driven emotion.

Adrenaline, the hormone of the fight-or-flight response is also a critically useful and important adjunct to good performance in any sport — but most participants get their dose of adrenaline from the excitement of the game itself. Purposefully getting "angry" is one way to stimulate an adrenaline rush — other ways are: becoming frightened, becoming enthusiastic, feeling threatened and pressured, exercise, and even by drinking coffee! Perhaps the most natural way to get that old adrenaline circulating is by simply doing a vigorous warm-up session — jumping jacks, lunges, a fast jog around the building and the adrenaline starts pumping.

But what about that other aspect of competition — of purposefully meeting another person and seeking to outdo their best performance? Does that make the op-

ponent look bad, decrease his or her self-esteem? Cause
them to feel sad?

Some of the thoughts lurking in the back of many
women's subconscious minds include: I'll hurt them.
They won't like me. It's not right to attack someone. I
shouldn't try to look better than someone else. My
mother wouldn't act like this in public... Oh, how we are
bent on personal sabotage! These ideas, you'll notice,
have nothing to do with the sport of fencing itself —
they have to do with the appearance of aggression.

A woman selflessly defending her children or the poor
and weak against an attacker — well, she's a tiger, a god-
dess of protection and power. She appears very aggressive, yet we admire that woman! Even so, it is the same
urge to fight and overcome that underlies all competitiveness — the urge to improve, to win, to succeed. As a
culture, we admire aggression in women if it is the result of pressures upon her, but discourage aggression if
it is only a spontaneous urge.

I want to clarify that this urge, this desire, is a human
trait, not just a male or female one. Its presence in individual people varies from near-zero incidence to near-
100 percent presence, although most of us are willing to

I signed up for fencing when I was a student at the University of Southern California in 1971. There, the fine
Hungarian sabre master, Dr. Francis Zold, wanted to see
what I could do. I remember lunging ... and lunging ...
and lunging... as he backed across the gymnasium floor,
leading me while he gruffly intoned, "LONG lunge, LONG
one." By the time this torture session was over — me
gasping and struggling to remain on my feet — Dr. Zold
pronounced me, slow. But, he said, "speed isn't everything — you can outsmart your opponent."
After class, I went to the showers ... and promptly fainted
dead away, out cold on the tile floor. Following that social embarrassment (geez, Zorro *never* fainted), I made a
BIG mistake: I dropped the class.

be competitive when needed and willing to be laid- back the rest of the time. Typically, we think of competitiveness as a masculine trait, a primitive caveman desire to win all the prizes, kill the biggest elk, bring home the bacon, inhabit the largest cave, amass the greatest mound of gold.

Some men, though, have no desire to compete — the laid back Type B personalities who just want a nice meal and a warm place to sleep, and they're happy. The Type A personalities are driven to distraction by the urge and are happy only when they are dominating and winning over some hapless opponent, even at checkers, even while driving in Sunday traffic.

It's the same thing with the female of the species. Some are content with where they are and have neither desire nor need to move assertively into another person's space. Others need the interactions with others and their own environment, a need for tension or intense conflict, or the emotional extremes of winning and losing, in order to really feel alive.

Neither extreme is necessarily a better version of female personality — there's a time and place for everything. On the fencing strip, that competitive urge can be a benefit. It allows you to make use of your own best abilities and to achieve a maximum performance. But off the strip, say, waiting in line at the supermarket while your toddler is trying to grab candy from the displays, and the customer in front of you fumbles for their checkbook — well, the competitive urge is pretty unpleasant when it kicks in right then.

The important thing to remember with competitiveness: like any psychological state, there are times when it is appropriate and times when it is plain wrong. Women athletes sometimes carry a mistaken notion that their athletic prowess represents women everywhere to an uncaring, unfeeling male-dominated world.

Not so. There is nothing to prove on the fencing strip,

no one to convince of anything. You are out there only for a single purpose — to touch the opponent with your weapon according to a carefully prescribed set of rules, in a way that simulates the point-contact of a real swordfight. That, alone, is hard enough without carrying the burden of feminism or women's rights or any other political sloganeering on your back. The intense focus of thought, of effort, of movement, of adaptation, of adjusting to your opponent's skill, of bettering your own abilities — this is competition refined to its highest form. You don't have to win in order to compete successfully — that's just the icing on the cake. When you go out to fence, all you have to do is fence to the best of your ability.

Over time, you'll probably find (as many of us have), that you spend most of your effort competing against yourself — against your own learned restrictions, against your body's mechanics, and against your habits and fears. This is the real competition in fencing or, indeed, in any athletic event.

Important Issue Number Three: Fear

You see it most often with adolescent women — girls, really — who are exposed to the pointy-end of their opponent's weapon for the first time: cold fear.

Yes, we know that the opponent's sword has a blunt point; that the padding on our chest and the metal over our face is solid and provides plenty of protection, that the fencing master has control over his weapon and doesn't have any intention to actually damage you ...

But at the same time, that sudden movement of an apparently sharp object toward your body triggers a nearly-instantaneous reaction: it's going to hurt me. Muscles tighten, breathing becomes sharp and fast, your eyes close, you pull your arms inward and one leg up to shield the target area ... and lose control of your own weapon, your ability to respond, and your common sense!

In less-serious instances and with more mature women, you might find yourself twisting away from the incoming point, trying to dodge the weapon, thrusting your back hand forward. The result is the same: you lose control of your weapon and forget to protect yourself with steel.

This problem, brought to fencing either innately or through some prior experience with a threatening situation, can only be overcome one way: the behavioral psychologist's technique called "flooding." You must immerse yourself in the situation that causes the fear, until you fear it no longer.

Here's how. Put on your fencing gear, and ask a fellow fencer to lunge against you — use you as a target. Get into an en garde position, and take it! Make no moves for defense — if you have to, start with your eyes closed, then open them after 20 or 30 touches. When one friend tires out, ask another one to keep up the attacks.

Most women are completely relieved of the fear of touches after as little as three to ten minutes. For others, a couple of sessions of being touched repeatedly relieves the fear. You find out, really and truly, that the opponent's sword cannot harm you. Will you be surprised at how different you feel afterwards?

The flip side of the fear coin is a complicated one: *the fear of failure.* We want to perform well, we want to win our bouts, sometimes *so* powerfully, that we simply can't tolerate the idea of *not* winning. There's always a chance that we might not win, so for some women the emotionally-safest course is to perform at a sub-peak level. These women purposefully hold themselves back from making a strong touch, a direct attack, or even of physically working at their "flat out" level. In effect, this is a kind of psychological "playing it safe" routine. Afterwards, they can always say to themselves, "Well, I really wasn't trying my hardest, so it's okay that the other person beat me."

This *fear of failure* is probably one of the most insidious stumbling blocks a woman fencer can face. Rather than doing anything that might fall short of perfection, new fencers might hold back, playing it safe, basically doing nothing at all. Of course, this dooms her to failure for sure. She might attempt one or two simple actions she feels relatively comfortable with, but she's afraid that any experiment will fail — and, not surprisingly with that attitude, it frequently does.

In a tournament, that same fear of failing, of losing officially, turns into paralyzing tension — which translates into either wild overreaction or a withdrawal into a total defensive shell. In both instances, the fencer just stands there, waiting nervously for something to happen. It usually does: she loses.

In learning to fence, you need to be prepared to make mistakes. You *will* make mistakes. Everyone does. Do not let yourself be overly concerned. This is not only a rite of passage in your growth as a fencer, it's also an opportunity to learn more about your own body, your skills, your determination, and your natural inclinations. Become a scientist, mentally step back and watch your own actions: is that woman (your fencer self) holding back? Is she making clean, sharp actions? Is she really working the hardest she can?

Playing it safe doesn't teach you anything. Just fence. Try everything in the book. Nothing is totally easy in fencing — real mastery takes constant input. You will only have a chance of becoming a real fencer if you are willing to continue to put yourself on the line.

Important Issue Number Four: Sweat

I vividly remember my mother telling my 7-year-old self, "Ladies don't sweat; they perspire." I'm not sure if she was just trying to help me distinguish between some interesting semantics or trying to encourage me to give up my tomboyish ways, but the end result was that "sweating" became a no-no.

Of course, everybody sweats. There are sweatglands in nearly every square inch of your skin, each beneficially designed to pump out a minute amount of body fluid onto the surface of your skin with only one goal in mind: keep you cool. Without the ability to sweat, to cool your body, you would die. It's that simple. During any athletic experience — yes, even just running to catch the bus! — your body will generate a certain amount of sweat. In moderately warm weather, you may sweat away a pint of fluid quite easily, even without noticing it. After a hard workout on the fencing strip (wearing that nice, thick, warm fencing uniform), you could actually lose several pounds of fluid — each pound equal to about a pint of fluid. Your uniform is soaked and damp, your hair is stuck to your head, and your once-crisply white leather fencing glove is turning gray from the wetness of palm and wrist.

This is a good thing. You'll look just as damp, hot, and sweaty as everybody else in the salle.

Be sure to replace those lost fluids by drinking plenty of extra water or electrolyte replacement drinks (Gatorade, PowerAide, or similar stuff). Fruit juices are okay (but add excess sugar and calories), but soda pops are not such a good idea — too much sugar and caffeine that further depletes fluids by stimulating the kidneys to release liquids.

Important Issue Number Five: Feeling Stupid

Or incompetent or hopeless. Everyone, on their first experiences with fencing, feels like they have six knees that are all going in different directions.

The position of the lunge is initially awkward, the coordination of arm movements, the development of speed, all take effort and time to come together. We all intellectually know this, but somehow expect that it won't apply to me. And when it turns out that it does apply to yourself, many women's first reaction is to think: "There must be something wrong with me. Everybody else can do this without looking like they're totally uncoordinated. Everybody else isn't gasping after the first three lunges. Everybody else is having a good time, and I'm not."

It doesn't even matter where this negative emotional baggage originated — childhood experiences, difficult parenting, trauma, past endeavors — it makes no difference. Today is where the problem is operating, and that's where you can tackle it.

First, recognize that this self-defeating idea is just a feeling about reality — the feeling itself isn't reality. You may feel stupid, but that doesn't make you stupid.

Second, realize that this feeling is a reaction — a sudden thought triggered by a situation. It isn't something you deliberated and then came to a conclusion about. Fast reactions are good when you're driving on a slick roadway, but not so good when you're making decisions about your personality or future. That's when some reasoning is called for!

Instead of a *reaction* to a feeling, look for a *response* to the feeling. Here's how that's done:

Situation: You try a lunge for the first, second or twentieth time. You're wobbly, unable to keep your balance, and have trouble pulling back into the en garde position.

Reaction: Sheesh, I'm so uncoordinated, I can't even stand up. I was never good at sports. Everybody is laughing at me. What's the use?

Response (Better!): Wow, I'm really uncoordinated. I guess those years of working at a desk have let my muscles and balance get rusty. I've learned how to do new things before. If I just take my time and practice this stuff, I'll get it eventually.

See how different these outcomes are? You might even notice a difference in your attitude after merely reading the response.

Third, watch for these self-defeating reactions. If you find yourself beginning to feel down — any time, any where — there's a negative reaction going on somewhere in your thoughts. Trade in that reaction for a response.

A beginner learning the ropes

Cognitive psychologists have identified 12 distinct thinking mistakes — and each one of us will bring our own favorites to the fencing strip. If you are alert to these momentary slips — that is, if you notice that your mood changes and becomes negative, sad, self-deprecatory, upset, angry, troubled. Well, check and see if you're beating yourself up with one of these thinking mistakes.

Twelve Mistakes of Thinking

1. *All-or-nothing*: Looking at a situation as only black or white, with no shades of gray. Example: "If I don't win this tournament, I'm a total failure."

2. *Catastrophizing*: Looking for the worst possible outcome, without considering other more likely outcomes. Example: "I'll lose this bout, and my entire fencing career will be ruined."

3. *Discounting the positive*: You tell yourself that positive experiences or actions don't count. Example: "I got two solid touches against a better fencer, but it was just luck."

4. *Emotional reasoning*: If you feel something, it must be true, ignoring evidence to the contrary. Example: "Even though I've learned a lot about fencing and have improved my skills dramatically, I don't win all my bouts. I feel like a loser."

5. *Labeling*: Putting a fixed label on yourself or others, when evidence could lead to a better conclusion. Example: "I'm a klutz."

6. *Magnification/minimization*: When you take a negative experience and use that to blot out any positive side to it. Example: "Losing that bout proves I'm incompetent. Just because I won another one doesn't mean I've got any skill."

7. *Mental filter*: Paying attention to the trees instead of the forest. Example: "I couldn't do the lunge fast enough (even though I won the bout)."

8. *Mind reading*: You think you know what others are thinking, even without considering more likely possibilities. Example: "She's thinking I'm fat and slow."

9. *Overgeneralization*: Making a sweeping negative conclusion that goes far beyond the current situation. Example: "Because I felt uncomfortable during my first fencing lessons, I don't have what it takes to fence well."

10. *Personalization:* You decide that other people's behavior is because of you, rather than considering other possibilities. Example: "The fencing master was curt to me because I'm stupid."

11. *"Should" and "must":* A fixed idea of how you or others are supposed to behave, and overestimation of the negative outcome if these expectations aren't met. Example: "It's terrible that I lost that bout. I should always be able to win."

12. *Tunnel vision*: You only see the negative aspects of a situation. Example: "I can't do any fencing right. I'm clumsy and dumb, and slower than everybody else."

One of the really fine things about learning fencing — or learning anything, really — is what brain scientists have just discovered: when you learn something new, especially if it involved physical activity, you actually increase your number of new brain cells! Learning, it was found, triggers certain neural cells called "stem cells" to begin to transform into various other types of brain cells. This means that you actually *are buildling your brain power*, every time you practice fencing!

This may help explain why old-time fencing masters survived to astonishing old ages (Nick's master, Ralph Faulkner, lived to be 96 and taught fencing until two weeks before his death) *and* kept their mental faculties intact as well.

And you thought fencing was just a sport!

Important Issue Number Six: Fencing Versus Everything Else

Women in today's society have a rather peculiar problem: believing that they must be able to be wife, mother, employee and homemaker, all rolled into one attractively dressed and professionally coiffured bundle. In the "un-enlightened" days of our grandmothers, it was enough for a woman to simply be a career girl (or whatever) — no one expected a woman to do all the rest along with it. In fact, it was typical that when a career girl settled down as a homemaker, she would drop the job like a hot rock.

Was that a case of oppression by a patriarchal social system? Or a common sense understanding about how much one woman can accomplish in a day? I'll leave it for the historians to hash that one out.

Meanwhile, my 24-hour day is so packed with important and necessary things to do ("Pick up the kids at the bookstore," "Drive 250 miles to a seminar," "Don't forget to get flowers for that friend in the hospital," "Oh, no - not chicken again tonight!" "The vacuum cleaner is buried under the clothes I meant to wash," "The dog hasn't had a bath since 1994," and "I've got a 60-page paper to write before Friday.") that it seems like there isn't time in the day for what NEEDS to be done — much less for fencing.

In consequence, American women are finding themselves more likely to suffer from the diseases of stress — high blood pressure, digestive problems, headaches, heart disease — than their grandmothers were. It's hardly any wonder why, since the high-pressure on-the-go lifestyle is nonstop stress. Somehow, we've stepped onto a very fast treadmill and don't seem able to climb down.

Where does fencing, or any sport for that matter, fit into this picture?

Physical exercise may be just the ticket for reducing the hazards of daily stress. Aerobic exercise, the kind that requires you to breathe deeply and consistently for a good 30 minutes or longer, makes significant changes in metabolism, improves immune function, burns off the accumulated stress, and gives you a chance to forget about the problems of the day. People who exercise — even just walking or gardening — for 30 minutes, three to five times a week have significantly lower chance of suffering a heart attack than those who don't.

Exercise, by itself, has enough ability to provide real health rewards. But, with fencing, there's more. When you are fencing, or even practicing fencing your center of focus closes down to nearly a single point — your opponent's target area, for example. Concentration sharpens. Hand-eye-coordination improves. The action of lunging drives your heart, lungs and blood vessels to perform their best. Your timing becomes quicker, more decisive. By facing an opponent, you learn strategy, timing, patience, lightness of touch, anticipation, technique, skill, how to lose gracefully, how to win without being overbearing. By joining a fencing school or club, you meet and share experience with people you might not know otherwise: physicians, housewives, attorneys, aviators, childcare workers, authors, firefighters, clerks, cattle ranchers, dancers, and people of all sorts, all brought together by a common interest in the blade. You'll passionately argue issues you never imagined anyone cared about: whether a straight arm attack is better than a bent-arm one, who the best fencer in your group is, whether fencing with electric equipment distorts the traditions of the weapons.

All of this will change you in ways that no one can fully predict. You will have greater self-confidence, but how that more assured you will show herself, we can't say.

Perhaps, this you will look at her busy schedule and decide to write down the most critical items that she truly *must* do — and then notice that some things can be done by other family members, or done at a different location or time, or just dropped entirely. Maybe she will discover that it's morally, socially and emotionally okay to take time for herself, a few hours every week — especially since it makes her a more fascinating and healthy person to be with. Wouldn't that be an interesting change?

Important Issue Number Seven: Overdoing It

It's the flip side of not having enough time: committing too much time, too much energy, and too much of your life to fencing (or anything else).

Our society values athletes who dedicate their existence to the pursuit of medals and awards. Run faster, lift more weight, get more touches, and you become the darling of a very monied set of humanity (commercial sponsors).

The end result of this single-minded focus is seldom the personal happiness and well-being that you'd expect.

American fencing, at the top elite levels, hasn't had quite the promotion and intense sponsorship that track or gymnastics or even women's basketball has — which has somewhat protected women fencers from the kinds of pressures other athletes face to this point. However, times are changing. Coaches whose own careers hinge on producing winners can let their enthusiasm spur on women athletes to real performance highs ... and real emotional and physical destruction (more on this in the Special Concerns Chapter).

Of course, on the level of friendly competition, women fencers seldom feel driven to make lifestyle-hazardous decisions just to win a bout or to enter a tournament, but it does happen. This is the point where you need to be alert to yourself and your own motivations. Ask yourself these questions:

Does fencing make it easy for me to avoid other responsibilities (work, home, relationships)? If you find this to be the case, then fencing is becoming a dodge, a way out of normal life. Fencing itself probably isn't the real problem — it's that you're too stressed, too confused, too anxious, or too afraid to deal with the real problem you're avoiding, and you're letting fencing do the avoiding for you.

Am I using fencing as an excuse for certain behaviors? More often than not, fencing helps develop a sense of self-confidence and assurance — but, some women take that assurance to a next step into brash, harsh, egomaniacal arrogance. It's unpleasant to be around and can't feel that good to the woman who does it since it drives people away. If your goal is to alienate everyone you know, this is the way to do it.

Do I feel like I have to absolutely perfect one movement (say, a lunge or a disengage) before learning anything else? While it's good to recognize when you're able to perform an action in its best form, it isn't necessary to be perfect all the time. Given the nature of the human body and fencing itself, it probably isn't even possible. If you find yourself struggling with overdoing "perfection" at any stage of your learning, you might actually be trying to prevent moving on. "I can't get this disengage right (so I don't have to bout yet)" might be the kind of message you're actually sending.

Do I spend more time on repetitive drills than on fencing? There are real benefits to drilling certain movements and actions from time to time. Just as a ballet dancer will go through a series of positions and movements to warm up, stretch out, and prepare for a performance, a good fencer needs to go through the motions of the sport for a few minutes. Repetitive drilling that absorbs an hour, two hours, an entire session, or that is carried on day after day, though, *won't* help your fencing. It might actually ruin your skills by converting thought responses into mere reactions. If you find yourself doing this, you might be using the drills as a method of ignoring other problems in your life.

These basic questions — and other factors, discussed in the next chapter — can help you identify if you're overdoing fencing. In reality, though, fencing itself isn't the root of the problem; fencing is the tool you're using to keep other life problems at arm's length. Sometimes this is a good strategy for dealing with personal problems (ignore it and it will go away), and sometimes this is the worst possible decision because the problem gets worse when it isn't addressed.

Overdoing it? Ask yourself what fencing is keeping you from — and *that* might be the real problem.

Important Issue Number Eight: Friends and Family

We may stand on the strip facing our opponent without benefit of friends or family to help us fight our bout, but they're always there in the back of our thoughts. Small children wonder why Mommy goes away some nights and comes back flushed and tired; husbands wish somebody else would do the laundry or clean up the floor when the wife is at fencing; parents worry that the (extremely rare) injury from a broken blade will happen to their daughter; and friends look you up and down when you tell them you're taking up fencing — and you can practically hear them thinking, "It'll never last!"

No one can decide for you whether fencing will be a lifetime activity or just a short association. Skeptical and well-meaning friends may have their own reasons for discouraging or encouraging you; family members may be innocently concerned about their own needs or if Mommy is going to totally abandon them; and parents are supposed to worry — that's their job. But this doesn't mean you need to give up your own interests and activities.

Your time away from the family can be a break for them, too.

Another factor that can become a consideration is the effect of fencing on the family budget. If you need to give up work time in order to fence, there might be a decrease in your paycheck. Buying fencing equipment isn't as expensive as acquiring golfing supplies, but the dollars can easily mount up. The spouse might resent an expense from which he doesn't receive a direct benefit.

An effective strategy, something like a situational-counterparry, is to negotiate with the people who will be affected by you going to fencing. For the husband or boyfriend or significant-other: "I'll trade you *me getting two nights of fencing a week* for *you getting two nights of incredibly fancy homecooked meals* or *you getting two nights of your favorite sports programs on TV*" and so on. It doesn't hurt to mention that the spouse might find fencing pretty interesting, too!

For the young children: it won't harm them for mom to be away for a couple hours during the week, especially if Daddy, grandparents or an emotionally-close friend stays with them.

For doubtful parents: show them your protective gear. Let them try on your mask, your glove, your chest protector, and feel the weight of your jacket. It might help them to know that injuries in fencing are remarkably few — only a handful of deaths worldwide in the past 50

Getting hit

years (all at Olympic levels), MUCH fewer than even high school soccer or football or weekend skiing. The most common fencing injuries are muscle strains and sprains... hardly the stuff to fuel parental anxiety.

Balance between your obligations as a family member, and your interests as a maturing woman can be achieved with constructive strategizing. Remember to offer the family something besides "I won't be here" — give them a reason to be happy for your new adventures!

THE PHYSICAL SIDE

Conditioning and Nutrition

In a turnabout that surprised quite a few old-time fencers, *Time* (July 17, 2000) reported a resurgence of interest in fencing, especially among young women. While it probably shouldn't be surprising that such a fascinating pursuit has found converts, it comes on the heels of years of decline in general fitness throughout the U.S. with the "couch potato" syndrome ushering in increasing weight, type II diabetes (the adult-onset variety), and an all-time national high in consumption of fastfoods and microwaveable foods.

Along with this, *Health*[2] magazine touts fencing as a source of "strength, grace, and mental stimulation" — and even *Heart & Soul*[3] magazine lists fencing as one of six sports for ultimate fitness! They write, "Fencing is extremely satisfying, not to mention strenuous. It demands coordination, balance and precision, and will sharpen your agility, strength and speed."

These reports and others bring with them a springtime quality to the entire fencing world, a sense of rejuvenation and growth that it hasn't seen for decades. Perhaps this is only one small part of the pendulum swing that appears to be taking place in many fields — a move toward quality over quantity, substance over fluff, and skill over hackerhood. We certainly hope so. As a reader of this book, you're part of this exciting time and can

> If you've ever heard the expression, "No pain, no gain," we urge you to immediately forget it, to purge it forever from your memory banks. Pain is quite simply something to be avoided. Too often in the quest for fitness, people buy into the mistaken notion *that exercise has to hurt to help*.[1]
> — Michael Eades, M.D. and Mary Dan Eades, M.D.

add your contributions to the fencing world!

The physical and health side of fencing can seem daunting at the outset. The first time you see experienced fencers bouting, they look incredibly fast and agile — attributes you may feel you are lacking! But no one is born with a foil in her hand; all these things can be learned by practice and patience.

This chapter is a complex one. It is going to cover conditioning (exercise, diet) and mind-training (visualization). Our focus is on developing you to your personal highest level of fitness — the level you wish to achieve, not some mystical, magical state of perfect health or ideal athletic form. Every woman has her own needs, her own life, and her own ideals — and that is where fencing needs to fit for you. Some women are suited to become full-time athletes, with strong naturally-agile bodies and intense dedication and focus on movement. Other women are more leisurely in their sport interests — they want a challenging pastime that brings out their best but fits within their schedule. Others just want to go out and mix it up with other fencers. Some just wish to take lessons and join in group work as a form of exercise and prefer to avoid bouting itself. All of these alternatives are acceptable and respectable; you only need to do as much as you want to.

At the same time, I'll be presenting new research and cutting-edge discoveries in diet and nutrition, along with techniques for mind-training that really do affect your health and performance.

Exercise, Conditioning, and Why

Preparation for fencing is the same as preparing for any kind of physical workout — a brief 5-10 minute period of stretching, bending, lunging and point work will loosen up all the muscles and make them warm and ready for the bout or lesson to come.

When you begin stretching and limbering up, keep in mind that *all* movement can be a form of conditioning if you focus on what you're doing. Begin stretching just as if you were getting up in the morning — a long, clean stretch with your arms high over your head. Feel the lengthening of your muscles all along your back, down the backs of your legs. Make all your movements slow and deliberate. Concentrate on how every muscle, joint, and tendon feels.

Point your toes, and flex them up toward your knees. Squat on your haunches, then extend yourself to standing. Lean to left and right. Twist your torso. Raise and lower each shoulder. Extend your arms and swing them in small circles. Don't be alarmed if you hear your neck or back crack: it shows you're limbering up.

Stretching is most effective when done slowly, like a cat stretches. Don't bounce (bouncing causes micro-tears in muscle fiber); don't push beyond the point where you begin to feel pain. If you get short of breath or feel dizzy, lay down flat on the floor immediately. Stretching should feel good itself, and make you feel better!

After stretching, performing several lunges will start your blood pumping vigorously and further exercise your legs. Work on perfecting your form, improving your speed, or focusing your point-control. Five minutes of lunging with your weapon and touching a small target will give you an excellent warm-up and good overall workout. At this point, typically, you'd move on to a few conventional exercises to refine and sharpen your movements.

Always begin any exercise session with stretching and

Always important: stretching and warming-up

warm-ups. This will help prevent sprains and strains, as well as making the entire experience more pleasurable.

Conditioning Concepts

For fencers who wish to use the sport to further improve their physical state, there are definite methods of conditioning that can be useful for fencers when they are not on the strip. Bear in mind the obvious. If you want to be a good skier, the best way to do it is to ski. If you want to be a good baseball player, there's no better way than to get out and play baseball.

The best conditioning for fencing is to go and fence. All other conditioning plans are simply adjuncts, aids to physical development. You can increase your body's ability to endure hard workouts by jogging, dancing, or even by doing wind-sprints, but the only way to improve your point control is to use your foil. The best way to speed up your lunge is to lunge fast and firm. The finest method to increase your focus on the opponent's target area is to fence!

With that in mind, it's clear that sometimes you can't fence (salle's closed, weather is too rough, broke your last foil blade, boss wants you to work late, etc.), but you want to keep in shape anyway. We're suggesting here some physical conditioning systems that can be done at home, on vacation, or for very little cash outlay that improve muscle tone, cardiovascular endurance, and general fitness.

Cardio-pulmonary Conditioning

Your heart (cardio) and lungs (pulmonary) are the critical components of a good conditioning program. Clearly, unless your heart can successfully pump a large volume of your blood that has been well-saturated with oxygen by passing through your lungs, you can't exercise! Common symptoms of an insufficient supply of oxygenated blood in your circulatory system include gasping, shortness of breath, inability to breathe deeply, feeling of dizziness, spots before your eyes, light-headedness, and so forth. If you've had these experiences while exercising, you should check with your doctor to be certain there isn't some underlying symptom causing the problem.

For most healthy adults who have spent a few years in a sit-down job, these kinds of symptoms are very brief and short-lived, occasionally present during the first days of a new exercise program. These kinds of symptoms then can represent your body's protests against moving too fast too quickly. Your heart and lungs are not yet able to keep up with the pace.

An excellent tool to check on your cardiopulmonary fitness is your pulse rate. You can determine your pulse by putting light pressure over the radial artery in your wrist (as shown on page 91)or at your carotid artery in your neck (as shown on page 92).

You may need to stop moving and stand still in order to feel the pulse wave. Always use your first two fingers to feel for your pulse, and don't use your thumb. The thumb has its own pulse, and it's too easy to count extra beats when feeling with your thumb.

The table on page 93 shows target rates for typical ages. When exercising, it is generally recommended that you keep your heart rate within the limits shown. This is a calculated heart rate based on your age and doesn't take into account such factors as your weight, your build, or your body's fat-composition, so these are necessarily general numbers.

If you wish to calculate a pulse rate for yourself, here is the formula to use: 220 - (your age) = maximum heart rate

Never try to achieve your maximum rate" during a workout. Typically, if you keep your heart rate at 70-80% of maximum, your workout will achieve the most cardiovascular benefit. So, if your age is 35, your absolute maximum heart rate would be 220 - 35 = 185. (If you find yourself getting close to your maximum rate, return to a slow walk and then rest for 10-20 minutes.) Your peak performance rate would be 70% x 185 (.70 x 185) = 130 beats per minute. A pulse rate in your peak performance range will provide the most benefits for your exercise time.

Walking

A good basic exercise that is both inexpensive and easy to do is walk. It sounds too simple, too basic, but even a stroll around the block will help build cardiovascular endurance.

When my children were toddlers, I spent almost all my time indoors in one or two rooms. So much so that it even became a chore just to walk outside to the mailbox. I actually found myself panting when climbing up a mere 12 steps to the upper floor of our house. After beginning a walking program which consisted of taking 30

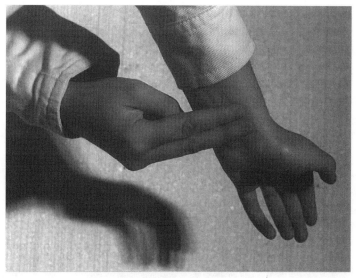

Taking the radial pulse

minutes to cover a mile (a very slow mile!), I found that this simple process gave me sufficiently improved endurance that I could jog to the mailbox and up those steps with ease. Doesn't sound like much, but it was a big deal to me at the time!

This simple activity eventually led to us acquiring a treadmill for use when the weather was unfriendly. The daily mile lengthened into two, and then three. This not only benefits your entire cardiovascular system, it also keeps your metabolism running at a somewhat higher rate, helps peel unnecessary pounds off, and provides exercise for those major weight-bearing muscles and bones. On occasion, I'll jog a portion of the time.

If you've been out-of-shape for awhile, the most important thing to keep in mind is this: don't overdo. Keep track of your pulse by pausing and checking it for a good minute, and if your heart rate is over 10 percent higher than the listed peak performance level, slow down or rest! It probably took you several years to get out of shape – so don't expect to get back into shape overnight.

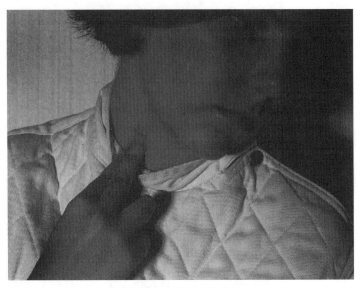

Taking the carotid pulse

It's a fact, you will only continue any exercise, such as walking or fencing, if it is enjoyable — a pleasure rather than a punishment. If you need to encourage yourself to exercise, include something pleasant at the end of the experience — a special treat such as buying a bouquet of flowers, taking a leisurely shower, special soaps or fragrances, reading a novel — whatever acts as a reward for performing the activity (avoid food rewards!). One neophyte exerciser paid herself $2 every time she finished a mile walk, and earned enough in a three month period to afford a special weekend vacation at a mountain retreat — one that had miles of beautiful forest hiking trails!

Jogging

Jogging, a slow trotting run, is another way to keep the heart and lungs in good shape. It's a little bit harder on the knees, ankles, and hips than walking, but there may be some real cardiovascular benefits to increasing the speed (and distance) covered during a workout. Jogging will provide

Age	Maximum Rate *(do not try to reach maximum rate)*	Target (Peak Performance) Rate
20	200	140
25	195	136
30	190	133
35	185	130
40	180	126
45	175	122
50	170	119
55	165	115
60	160	112
65	155	108
70	150	105
75	145	101
80	140	98

greater capacity to your heart and lungs, useful if you find yourself in long competitions or having to compete against younger or more athletic fencers.

Ideally, you'd be better off jogging on a grass track, or area that is not on concrete walkways. This is because the impact from each foot hitting the ground — and passing that energy up your entire body — is decreased on a grass track, so that impact is much less intense than when you jog on concrete.

That brings us to shoes. If you decide to take up jogging, you *will* need a better-quality running shoe to protect your feet, ankles, knees and hips. We all have our favorite brands and styles (I prefer men's Nike crosstrainer, since my feet are so big!), but a good pair of joggers will have some traits in common:

♦ They fit well and don't cause blisters, corns, or pressure spots.

♦ They have a thick and flexible sole that both cushions your foot and bends to conform to your foot's shape easily.

♦ They support your foot laterally, that is, on both the outside edge and the inside edge. Some shoes sold as women's running shoes lack this lateral support. To me, this is a major failing of women's running shoes. When you jog, your entire weight transfers from foot to foot, so that each foot holds your full weight for a moment. In shoes without good lateral support, a slight cant or lean when that foot hits the ground can mean a rapidly twisted ankle — along with a hard fall to the pavement! My preference for cross-trainers, which have solid lateral extensions that resist this kind of problem, comes from lots of experience with running shoes (and collisions with the ground).

♦ They have a thick heel that cushions against heel strikes on the pavement.

Typically, you'd expect to spend between $50 and $100 for a good quality pair of shoes. Although this seems like a ridiculous amount of money to spend on shoes, you're actually investing in improved health, better movement, and avoiding injuries. Good shoes that fit well and support your feet are worth it!

Always wear socks when you jog — try different types to find which makes your feet feel most comfortable. For most recreational joggers, a pair of white cotton socks — either thick ones or lightweights — is the best type. Other women prefer a nylon variety; some like a silk sock next to the skin, covered by absorbent cotton or wool outer sock. Whichever version you find most comfortable, it should help protect your feet from wear spots, blisters, and chafing while wicking sweat away from the skin.

In addition, when you jog you need to follow basic safety advice:

♦ Don't wear headphones (that may distract you or make it difficult to hear car horns or other warnings).

♦ Don't jog alone or in isolated areas (no sense inviting trouble from unpleasant strangers).

◆ Wear loose-fitting clothing, and take off layers as you warm up.

◆ Don't jog at night or in dark areas.

◆ Wear reflective clothing patches even in day light.

◆ If you fall, stay down until you have assessed your condition — don't leap to your feet in embarrassment and try to disappear! Make sure ankles and knees are capable of carrying you home. If not, get assistance (taxi, police, EMTs, friends) to help you.

◆ Don't try to outrun loose dogs. Stop, make friends (if the dog is willing), or use pepper spray to discourage the aggressive ones.

◆ Don't overdo — start with no more than 30 minutes three to five times weekly or less if that leaves you feeling overtired or exhausted.

That last one, don't overdo, is probably the hardest one to stick by. Once you begin to feel pretty good about jogging, the tendency is to add a little bit more or go a little bit faster. However, going faster or farther isn't necessarily a benefit. You can actually begin to cause damage to your heart and muscles, weakening them rather than strengthening them, and bones begin to lose their calcium by excess exercising. Keep your pulse at the rate recommended earlier, and you'll be doing yourself the most good. You should be able to say a full sentence without gasping — such as "Yankee Doodle went to town, just to ride a pony" — and that shows you're getting sufficient oxygen for all your body's needs.

If you begin to experience pain in your ankles, knees, hips, or shooting pains in your calves, or any variety of chestpain, then you're overdoing it.

If you have chestpains, stop and see your doctor or an emergency room immediately. *DO NOT WAIT.*

For joint and muscle pain, give yourself a rest for several days until the pain is gone. Use ice-compresses immediately following the workout and warm packs after 24-hours have passed. If you begin to hurt again when you resume jogging, you're doing something wrong! A visit to your regular doctor or a sports physician will help resolve the problem.

Swimming

This sport is ideal for women who already have concerns about their joint strength, or who cannot tolerate the joint-pounding of jogging but still want an exercise that is more vigorous than walking.

Swimming, especially if it involves doing laps — back and forth swimming across the length of a pool — will develop your shoulder and arm muscles, giving women a more powerful upper body. This is the result of the motions used to propel yourself through the water — arm strokes of both the crawl (standard swimming technique taught at all swimming programs) and breaststroke (a wider and more lateral reach than the crawl) put both arms through a full range of motion. At the same time, your legs make a back-and-forth kicking motion.

In addition, the water helps to buoy-up your body, so the pounding of your full weight against a hard surface doesn't occur.

Unless you have a pool in your backyard, swimming can be a more expensive and time-consuming sport than either walking or jogging. You need to join a health-club that has a pool or find another facility that is available when you are ready to swim. You'll need a bathing suit — one that is non-restrictive and comfortable but won't float off (bikini-types are particularly bad for this). If you don't already know how to swim, you will probably wish to take lessons (one- or two-week courses are usually offered in the summer at YWCAs and other facilities).

While swimming is both fun and a cardiovascular benefit, it doesn't really strengthen your leg muscles (which you need for strong lunges), and it actually may increase the thin layer of body fat beneath your skin (as a protection against the cool water). If you find it difficult to hold your fencing weapon up in proper position for the full lesson, swimming might be an excellent way to strengthen those shoulder and upper-arm muscles to compensate.

Bicycling, Stair-steppers, Rowing

Bicycling for cardiovascular fitness has a long history — even back before people thought of bikes as fitness machines, and only saw them as a form of transportation. Bicycling principally uses the large muscles of the thighs, but using your legs in the vigorous pumping motion provides a benefit to heart and lungs, as well as the legs themselves.

Considerably more expensive than walking, jogging, or swimming, you will need a bicycle for this, a safe riding pathway (some cities now have bike paths), helmet, knee and elbow pads, and comfortable clothing. The bike should have reflectors on front and rear fenders, as well as a water bottle and center-mounted air pump for the tires.

The bicycle doesn't need to be an expensive racing model — in fact, a mountain bike is preferred for stability, utility, strength, ease-of-use, and comfort's sake.

Even though most bike-racers do their riding in a crouching position (to reduce wind-resistance and increase speed), this is not the most comfortable or safest position in which to ride. For good cardiovascular benefit, you need to sit upright with the handlebars at arm's length (so that you are able to control the bike without leaning forward). The seat should be adjusted high enough that you can almost fully extend your leg on the downward pedal stroke, and you need a wide seat that fully supports your bottom — not a narrow, hard racing seat. The racing seats have been shown to compress blood vessels (especially in men) and cause longterm fertility problems.

In a gymsetting, we can get the same benefit from stationary bikes without the risks of riding in traffic or falling. In addition, in a gym or home-style bike version, you can also see how far you've gone and possibly even your speed, depending on the extras that come with the bike itself. Once again, as with jogging, check your pulserate and keep it within the optimal range.

Bike riding is less stressful on the joints of the lower body, but doesn't provide any real exercise to the upper body — your arms don't get any workout at all.

Stair-steppers provide a vigorous cardiovascular workout in a fairly short and concentrated effort. They tend to protect those lower limb joints because each step is somewhat cushioned through the mechanism of the machine. As with bicycling, these devices tend to work only the lower body, though. Because using them can be pretty boring, some women lose interest in this system fairly quickly (I did). Other women find that they can bliss out and just keep stepping in rhythm to music or while watching TV. Adjust your stepper so that the first workouts are on the light or easy setting, so you can become accustomed to this approach. Move up to higher or harder settings as your pulse rate stabilizes in the correct range.

Rowing, either in an actual boat or on a rowing-machine, is a full-body workout that makes use of muscles of the back, the shoulders, and the large muscles of the legs. Muscles of the upper front chest aren't used as much, nor are the calves and feet. Surprisingly, the cardiovascular benefits of rowing are comparable to fast jogging — even though you are sitting down — simply because the entire body is involved in making the stretching and pulling movements on the oars. Joints throughout the body are protected from impact-damage, too.

I find rowing very soothing — the repetitive motion becomes regular and hypnotic, and sitting down nearly on the ground prevents accidental falls, so I can turn my brain off entirely while I'm doing it. Other women, though, report they found rowing as boring as I found stair-stepping!

Weight Training

Using weights — even a set of 1-pound hand-held dumbbells — has been the subject of much research and study lately. It's been shown that elderly (75 years and older) nursing home women who lift a one-pound weight for 10-15 minutes every other day begin to improve their muscle strength and bone mass — even if they haven't exercised in years. We are only beginning to understand the body's amazing regenerative and recouperative abilities.

Weight training is relatively inexpensive (a pair of 5-pound hand-held weights costs less than $10), and can be done at home or office, any time of the day or night. No special clothing is required, but comfortable old sweats work just fine. Hand-held weights will mostly focus training on your upper arms, chest, and back — just where you need it to help control your blade. Though there will be a moderate increase in your heart rate during a weight workout, weight training isn't really considered a type of cardiovascular training — its real benefit is to muscles, bones, and metabolism.

Best of all, you only need to use weights 2-3 times weekly for the maximum benefits — and no more than 30 minutes at a stretch. Even a 10-minute workout three times a week will strengthen muscles, build bones, and boost your metabolism (more on metabolism when we discuss nutrition).

For women who are in their middle years, weight lifting two or three times weekly helps prevent the   bone-loss of osteoporosis — plus streamlines and strengthens the muscles. For young women, weight lifting can provide that athletic look and strong build that typifies youth and health — as well as protecting your bones so that osteoporosis is even less of a problem in later life.

Researcher Miriam E. Nelson, Ph.D., author of *Strong Women Stay Young*[4], has developed a set of eight simple weight exercises that strengthen major muscles groups of the arms and legs. Her studies of women at various ages found that this very slow lifting of moderate weight produced remarkable benefits — from the expected improved strength, to the unexpected improved balance, better coordination, agility and confidence.

Her method involves slow lifting of fairly light weights — 2-3 pounds up to 20 pounds — three times each week. This includes lifting with the arms and using ankle weights to strengthen the legs. The key to doing the lifting correctly is to begin with a weight that can be hefted with a little effort and repeating for eight lifts, two times — a total of 16 lifts for each exercise. While lifting the weight, you count a slow 1-2-3, take a breath, and lower the weight to another slow 1-2-3 count. It hardly feels like effort at all, but the slow raising and lowering works the muscles continuously — and at the same time, develops real control over movement.

Dr. Nelson's eight exercises are explained in detail in her excellent book — we recommend it to women of all ages for strengthening and streamlining. At 48 years of age, I found that after only a few weeks of lifting 5 pound weights, I graduated up to 10-pounders — and then on up to 20 pounders all without any real physical distress. I also found that I could move up and down stairways with greater confidence (no more clutching the handrail!) and move furniture around the house when the mood struck me. Most amazing to me, perhaps, is that I can *feel* firm and resilient muscles in my arms and shoulders, where there once was soft, spongy areas!

If you choose Dr. Nelson's approach, you'll find that the cost of equipment is relatively low, compared to other sports. Each individual weight costs about $5, with a pair of 5-pound (adjustable) ankle weights about $15. You could begin with the purchase of two small hand weights and the ankle weights for a total of $25. The exercises themselves can be done at home, in front of the TV, or with friends.

Many health clubs and gymnasiums also feature lifting equipment and have advisors who can explain each system. Before beginning weights on your own, it's a good idea to acquaint yourself with the process of lifting — as well as deciding what outcome you want from your weights. If you want to bulk up, you can — and if you want to streamline you can do that, too. Different strategies and weight-adding systems produce different effects in your body.

Unintentional Exercising

Busy schedules and today's rushed lifestyle sometimes leave us wanting to exercise more, but not able to find the time. A little strategy can put more total workout time into your day with only a few small changes in your behavior:

1. Park the car a block farther away from work or at the far end of the supermarket or mall parking lot.
2. Take the stairs instead of the elevator.
3. Garden.
4. Put on your favorite dance music, and go to it while you clean house.
5. Walk the dog an extra time every day.
6. Stretch when having to reach, bend deeply when looking for something on a low shelf, do lunges when moving from side to side.

One fencing student, a grandmother, used her work time when making numerous photocopies to do some fencing exercises. She lunged to place papers on a shelf, did side-leg-lifts while standing in front of the machine, and used point control to mark on a wall-chart! Her boss, the dean of a college, happened to walk in during one of these workouts and said it was the most amazing photocopying technique he'd ever seen!

Keep in mind that exercise is exercise — your body makes use of all strengthening, lifting, moving, activities. Thirty minutes, three times a week, really can make remarkable changes and improvements in your health, even when those few minutes are spread out over several hours. Just a handful of small changes can make a big difference.

The Diet Question

It's no surprise that what you eat will have a big impact on your health. As a registered nurse, I was trained to follow (and teach) the official line — the food pyramid, with fats at the tiny pointy top, and grains and beans at the pyramid's bottom. America has been trained for almost 20 years to stick with this low-fat, high carbohydrate diet approach.

You know this system, probably by heart. Eat less fatty meats, avoid egg yolks, don't even breathe near butter, increase whole grains and beans, get plenty of fruits. Like me, you've probably followed various reduced-calorie diets over time or gone low-fat for extended periods.

For almost three years, I ate an extremely low fat diet, hovering between 8% and 10%. I lost 30 pounds initially. I ate huge amounts of fruits, vegetables, and whole-grain breads — but I was hungry all the time. After about two years, I noticed that my hair was extremely dry and lifeless — and getting thin! Two-and-a-half years into what I thought would be a lifelong eating plan, my joints began to ache and the weight started coming back. By the end of the third year, I'd gained back the 30 pounds (without changing my diet, mind you!) plus suffered from almost constant arthritis pain in my knees and hips.

Now, I'm only one person with this story — but it's becoming increasingly common. So common, in fact, that in 1996, at the Second International Symposium on Dietary Fats and Oil Consumption in Health and Disease (Southwestern University Medical School, Dallas, TX), the results of studies of low-fat eating confirmed it: low fat/high carbohydrate diets do NOT promote permanent weight loss — they contribute to weight gain and degenerative diseases! Most amazing of all, the March

1998 issue of the *American Journal of Clinical Nutrition* said, "Within the United States, a substantial decline in the percentage of energy from fat consumed during the past two decades has corresponded with a massive increase in obesity." In other words, *the less fat we ate, the fatter we got!*

How can this be, after all we've heard in the media about the benefits of cutting out fat from our lives? We have heard that all fat is bad, but animal-based fats are the worst — including the natural fat in meat, cheese and butter. We have also been told that red meat is full of evil chemicals and hormones and will probably clog our arteries; that whole-grains and beans together make a perfect protein that is just as good as meat nutritionally. That carbohydrates — breads, potatoes, pasta, natural sugars — are the high energy good foods that people have eaten since humans stopped being hunter-gatherers.

This has happened because the medical profession still doesn't know everything there is to know about the relationship between diet and health — and the media is not our friend when it comes to providing accurate information! One of these things that has been discovered relatively recently is the so-called syndrome X — a condition of high insulin (hyperinsulinemia) that appears to occur in some adults who follow the low-fat/high carbohydrate regimen. The high levels of insulin, produced by the pancreas to deal with blood sugar, seem to escalate and create further health problems over time — such as joint diseases, digestive problems, buildup of plaque in the arteries — all the things low fat was supposed to protect us from!

According to Diana Schwarzbein, M.D., an endocrinologist and author of the *The Schwarzbein Principle: The Truth About Losing Weight, Being Healthy and Feeling Younger,* here's what happens when you eat a low-fat/high carbohydrate diet:[5]

- When you eat a low-fat diet, you reduce your intake of protein and fat and increase your consumption of carbohydrates.
- The digestion of carbohydrates results in high levels of blood sugar being delivered to your liver.
- Excess blood sugar is converted to triglycerides (fat) and is used either as energy by the body or stored as fat.
- Continuing to eat an excess of carbohydrates sends a steady supply of blood sugar to the brain, keeping it satisfied.
- The absence of adequate proteins and fats in the diet forces the body to recruit these vital nutrients by breaking down its own muscle and bone mass.
- Years of eating low-fat will result in the interior rearrangement of your body's composition — muscle mass shrinks, bones will become less dense, and body fat will increase.

Dr. Schwarzbein is not alone in her contentions — the popular books *The Zone* by Barry Sears, Ph.D., and Drs. Eadeses' *Protein Power* also support the idea that low-fat/high-carb is not the way to improve health or lose weight.

In fact, there is an increasing amount of solid research that appears to show quite clearly that humankind's health began to degenerate dramatically after we began cultivating crops! Bioarcheologist Clark Spencer Larsen in his book *Skeletons in Our Closet* points out that our hunter-gatherer ancestors had better teeth, stronger bones, less diseases, and bigger muscles — while eating diets high in animal meats and fats, moderate in greens and leafy vegetables, and quite low in grains and fruits. This is almost the exact opposite of today's low-fat/high-carb approach.

This neolithic or stone-age diet has gained many converts from low-fat/high-carb eating, myself included.

Since following this program, my hair has become sleek and shiny, I am seldom hungry, I actually enjoy eating again, and I am losing weight — painlessly and without thinking about it — at the rate of about one pound per week. The real plus, though, is that I now have continuous and consistent energy throughout the day, and I sleep soundly throughout the night. My joints only hurt if I've overdone it at a workout — and give me progressively less pain over time!

What about cholesterol, though?

Drs. Eades (husband and wife team) and Dr. Schwarzbein all point out that their patient's cholesterol picture has improved, sometimes dramatically, when following this plan — mine is no exception. While consuming meat, eggs, sausage, fish, butter, cream, and assorted other forbidden foods, my cholesterol has come down over 25 points to 186, my HDL level (the good fats) has increased, while my LDL ("bad cholesterol) has gone down. My blood pressure has decreased by almost 40 points, to a normal level after being high for many years. This flies in the face of everything I learned in nursing school — but it has happened anyway!

And what about the purely sensual enjoyment of good eating?

We know that an over-focus on diet destroys the primal pleasure of a good meal — did I eat something I shouldn't? Will it make me fat/fatter? Will I die young because my arteries are filling with crud? Michelle Stacey, in her book *Consumed*[6] counters these fears, "Once we decide to give to food, its preparation and enjoyment, some time and what might even occasionally be called reverence, we may find that good food and good-for-you food is more likely to come from deep in the past — from ancient cultures and traditions that ... found their inspiration close to the land — than from the future, in the form of plasticized fat-free cheese and vegetable gums that glue together foods from which all natural moisture has been sucked out." Good food is food that nourishes both body and soul.

Each of the authors mentioned has their own way of presenting their plan, but Dr. Schwarzbein's very concise description here captures the essence of the stoneage plan:

◆ Don't skip meals. Five small meals a day are better than three.

◆ Eat real food that you could, in theory, pick, gather, milk, hunt or fish. Do not eat man-made carbohydrates [i.e. white sugar, flour, etc.]. Do not ingest artificial sweeteners. Do not eat processed packaged foods.

◆ Choose from the four nutrient groups at each meal [proteins, fats, nonstarchy vegetables, and carbohydrates, in that order!]. Eat all the good fats and proteins your body needs. Eat a variety of non-starchy vegetables. Eat carbohydrates according to your current metabolism and activity level.

◆ Taper off stimulants. Do not consume caffeine. Do not drink alcohol. Do not ingest stimulants.

◆ Avoid drugs. Do not take any over-the-counter medications. Ask your physician if you can stop any prescription medications.

There's a good deal more to Eades', Sears', and Schwarzbein's plans, though — so if you would like to understand the process in more detail, I recommend any (or all) of their books. As an example of how a typical day of eating would look under this plan, here's what I ate yesterday:

Breakfast:
two eggs, fried in butter, sunny-side up
two sausage links
1/2 slice whole wheat bread with butter
1/2 cup grapes
coffee with real cream

Lunch:
6 ounces of fish (herring snacks — my favorite!)
3 slices of "high fiber" rye crackers
butter
huge green salad with olive oil and vinegar
coffee with cream
Afternoon snack:
2 ounces of string cheese
handful of mixed nuts
coffee with cream
Dinner:
8 ounce T-bone steak, broiled
1 cup of steamed broccoli with butter
big salad, with real bleu-cheese dressing
1/2 cup of canteloupe
coffee with cream

Seems like a ridiculous amount of heart-clogging, weight-gaining food — but without the excess carbohydrates, our bodies do not store up excess fat. Best of all, for me this was a truly satisfying experience — real food, full of natural flavor and nutrition. (By the way, I know that I'm still on the caffeine train — which Dr. Schwarzbein indicates will increase insulin output. I'm working on it!)

On this eating plan, you may continue to have food cravings (bread, pasta, etc.) during the first week to ten days as your body adjusts away from the carbohydrate high of these foods. After that, you'll notice your energy level improving and your appetite changing. You can still have occasional sweet treats — but you'll notice afterwards that you retain water and feel groggy that makes you want to avoid the wrongly-called comfort foods like the plague! The whole concept of enjoying eating will be rekindled in you — and meals will no longer be a battle to control bad foods.

The effect on sports in general and fencing in particular is also quite remarkable: more energy, stamina, muscle strength, and better concentration. Dr. Sears' *The Zone* plan is especially aimed toward athletes, and includes studies of professional football teams and how changing from carb-loading before games to a protein-rich diet helped them play better and with less fatigue!

As a final thought on the diet issue, here is Mark Miller, who is both anthropologist and high profile chef:

"What's happened [in America] is that we don't have rituals with food, we don't understand the importance of food, we've lost the connection with farms, the connection of food with the land and the sea. People don't really want to discuss food. We don't have a food culture. It goes back to the Puritan days when people were put in the stocks for having spices in their kitchens. It's turning away from life ..."[7]

Enjoy food. Enjoy your life.

"Mind Training:" Understanding Visualization

A late 1999 issue of *American Fencer*, the United States Olympic Committee's publication for our sport, carried a brief report about one male fencer and how he prepared for a tournament bout. This individual used a technique that he had been taught — which he thought was visualization — to focus his thoughts. His visualization was to imagine himself the winner of the bout, repeating some affirmations ("I'm a great fencer" or some variation on that theme). By the way, he lost the bout.

The bout's outcome aside, whatever technique this fencer was using, it *wasn't visualization* — more like an imagined hopeful wish.

Successful visualization is a literal activation of specific areas of your brain. Recent research reported in the *American Journal of Psychiatry*[8] supported the long-controversial question of whether visualization during hypnosis was actually accompanied by physiological changes. The researchers said, in effect, that vivid changes in your personal experience during the visualization process are associated with changes in your brain that are typical of actual perception — that your brain, your mind, believes the visualization *is real!*

Clearly, just visualizing "I'm a great fencer" doesn't impart any useful information to your mind. It doesn't demonstrate how to make a good touch, move fast and confidently, or focus on your opponent's weaknesses. And using any technique that can be so easily overturned (the guy lost, so how can he be a great fencer?) only confuses the messages you send to your inner mind.

To understand how visualization works, we need to have a short overview of mental function. Briefly, we can imagine that we have two minds — an outer or conscious mind that is concerned with decisions, rules, order, and arranging factors in our lives. The conscious mind is characterized by an awareness of daily things, shared realities, events of the moment. We can think of the conscious mind as The Planner.

The inner mind, the subconscious, takes care of everything that is not in immediate conscious use — memories, breathing, heartbeat, muscle tension, all voluntary movement. This part of the mind doesn't plan anything — but it has an amazing ability to accomplish whatever plans the conscious mind sends to it. For example, when you turn a page of this book, you don't think, "Reach out with your right hand. Grasp the top of the page on the right between thumb and index finger. Move the page all the way to the left. Return right arm to resting position" — you just momentarily send a thought-image to your subconscious mind, "turn page." The rest of it, your inner mind takes care of on its own. We can call this part of the mind The Do-er.

Visualization is a process that focuses The Planner to train, teach, or demonstrate something to The Do-er. Here's a practice visualization that will help you understand how this works:

Picture in front of you a round, bright yellow lemon. Imagine that you reach out one hand and lightly touch it. Run your fingers over the slightly rough skin, the tacky, lightly oily surface, the bump on the end where the stem was. Imagine picking up this lemon. Feel the weight of it in your hand, its firm roundness. Bring it to your nose. Inhale and notice the pleasant, brisk citrus aroma. Imagine that you slice that lemon in half — the sudden sharp lemon smell, the juice dripping.

Many people can visualize this image so clearly, so strongly, that they also feel an increase in saliva in their mouth. The subconscious mind accepts the image as real, and brings about a change in your physical body that you would have if that lemon was actually right in front of you. Don't worry if you didn't have a dramatic response — you can learn to visualize, just as you can learn to drive, to walk, or to read.

To train your Do-er, you must first decide exactly what you wish to accomplish. Suppose you have noticed that when you lunge, you tend to pull back your arm (to not hurt your opponent). A visualization to control this problem might be to imagine yourself facing an opponent, no one in particular. Imagine you come *en garde*, feel the muscle tension in your legs, the weight of the weapon in your hand, your breath moving in and out past your mask. Now, visualize yourself lunging. Feel your legs move, watch your weapon extend forward, feel your arm turn into the correct position, feel the point contact your opponent squarely in the chest, the pressure on your hand, the spring of the steel. Return to *en garde*, feeling it, sensing your breathing, making this as vivid as you can in sight, smell, hearing and feeling.

Repeat this several times, over several days. The next time you fence, notice how differently your lunges feel, how you do contact more solidly, and with greater confidence. Your Planner will show your Do-er what to do, and the Do-er will bring it about.

In the same way, you can "practice" any aspect of fencing. The keys to success with visualization are:
1. Take a deep breath. Breathe out all tension. Close your eyes. Make the images, feelings, and ideas as vivid as possible — let your imagination be as colorful and creative as a child's.
2. Use all your senses to make this imagination real to your Do-er. Smell it, see it, taste it, hear it, feel it.
3. Be literal. Show your Do-er precisely what to bring about. Don't use vague or general ideas, such as "I want to win," or "I fence better than that other guy." See it, hear it, feel it, taste it, smell it!

The more you repeat the practice, the faster and more powerful the response will be. Remember: you are literally training your brain to perform a specific action in a certain way. Make sure you are telling yourself the correct information!

NOTES

1 Michael R. Eades, M.D. and Mary Dan Eades, M.D., *The Protein Power Lifeplan*, p. 296.

2 *Health*, March 2000, p.60.

3 *Heart & Soul*, April/May 2000, page 70.

4 Mirian E. Nelson, M.D. and Sarah Wernick , *Strong Women Stay Young*.

5 Diana Schwarzbein, M.D. and Nancy Deville, *The Schwarzbein Principle*, p. 139.

6 Michelle Stacey, *Consumed: Why American Love, Hate, and Fear Food*, p. 216.

7 Michelle Stacey, *Consumed: Why American Love, Hate, and Fear Food*, p. 199.

8 S.M. Kosslyn, W.L. Thompson, M.F. Costantini-Ferrando, N.M. Alpert, D. Spiegel, "Hypnotic Visual Illusion Alters Color Processing in the Brain." *American Journal of Psychiatry.* 157:8, 1279-1284.

SPECIAL CONCERNS OF THE WOMAN FENCER

There are issues that are of concern for the fencer of either gender and issues that are only of interest to woman fencers. This chapter will focus on these matters, with special emphasis on safety and health-promotion.

Common Injuries

Information on the types and severity of injuries typical to fencing is from Eric D. Zemper, PhD and Peter Harmer, PhD, "Fencing" in Epidemiology of Sports Injuries, edited by D. Caine, C. Caine, K. Lindner. Published by Human Kinetics, Champaign, IL, 1996, pages 186-95.

Both male and female fencers have an interest in avoiding any potential hazards, whether related to ordinary daily living or to the events of the fencing strip. Most of us are reasonably aware of the risks of our lives and lifestyles — we wear seat belts when we drive, avoid stepping on soap in the shower, and train our children to look both ways before crossing the street.

When practicing fencing, and especially when bouting, we wear a metal mask, a protective jacket, a glove, strong pants, and sturdy shoes. Even so, accidents happen.

One of the major fencing-related injuries is **heat exhaustion**. That protective jacket is generally layered over at least a T-shirt, but sometimes also over an underarm protector and a women's heavy plastic full-chest protector. The jacket collar extends up the neck nearly to the chin and closes securely. And that metal mask, as airy as it seems, actually seems to prevent free air movement over the fencer's face. All this adds up to a stifling uniform and a sweaty fencer. Add to this a warm to hot weather condition, vigorous exercise, and the setting is right for a *very hot* fencer.

Hot is different from heat exhaustion, though. A hot fencer removes her mask and unbuttons the top of her jacket when the bout is over, drinks several glasses of water or sportsdrink, and sits down to cool off. A fencer who is beginning to experience heat exhaustion might feel excessively hot, a bit dizzy, headachy, nauseated, or confused, or have bad muscle cramps — or might briefly lose consciousness.

Heat exhaustion is a serious condition. It can progress to heatstroke, a life-threatening overheating in which the body actually stops perspiring and the internal temperatures goes so high that brain damage, coma, or death may result. Heatstroke from fencing is *extremely rare*, but heat exhaustion can happen to anyone.

Your best protection against this potential problem is quite simple: drink plenty of fluids. Clear water is the best, followed by sportsdrinks that contain both sodium and potassium, electrolytes that your body sweats away and needs to have replaced through something you eat or drink. Soda pops are not a good choice — sugared sodas increase calories, increase fluid losses from your tissues, and don't really satisfy thirst. Sodas sweetened with artificial sweeteners may trigger headaches and further fluid losses. Just drink water, and plenty of it — even if you don't feel thirsty. Thirst occurs well after significant dehydration has taken place. For every hour of fencing during hot weather, try to drink a full quart of water — four full glasses. If you are sweating heavily, you won't feel much need to urinate in spite of the large amount you are drinking. Your body will process that water into sweat rapidly, doing just what it is supposed to do.

If you feel yourself getting overly-hot, nauseated, dizzy, or feel a headache come on rather quickly — cool off! Remove jacket and mask, sit down in a cool, drafty, shady place, and drink moderate (not icy!) water. Fencers who lose consciousness from overheating should be cooled and taken to emergency medical services for evaluation.

Relatively common injuries in fencing are *sprains* and *strains*. A sprain is a wrenching or twisting of a ligament or muscle near a joint, without accompanying bone damage. The most typical sprain, both on and off the fencing strip, occurs at the ankle. A strain is an injury of overexertion — you might strain your large leg muscles, quadriceps, by lunging repeatedly. The next day, you feel that strain as a heated, stiff feeling commonly known as sore muscles.

You can minimize the discomfort from either sprains or strains by following this strategy:

Sprains — immediately rest and elevate the affected area — get off your feet, put the twisted ankle up on a chair or bench. Apply a portable cold pack (available from pharmacies) or an ice pack (ice from cold drinks, placed in a plastic sandwich bag, is ideal), protecting your skin with a towel or flannel cloth — don't apply ice directly to the skin. Put ice on the injury up to 12 hours following the event. Don't move around any more than you have to. Overnight, apply a stretch-bandage to help support the joint. The next day, the injury should feel much better. If there is excessive bruising or any crepitus (creaking, popping, or a grating feeling and perhaps an increase in pain), you will need to have this examined by a physician and possibly have x-rays made.

Strains — Some of the discomfort from muscle strains occur as the result of lactic acid buildup in the tissues; some occurs from actual micro-tears of the muscle tissue itself. The approach that I have found most successful for myself is to follow the heavy workout with a very hot shower, plus one 500 milligram non-steroidal anti-inflammatory tablets (either aspirin or ibuprofen). The idea is to increase blood flow to the affected muscles by means of the hot shower, combined with the mild anti-clotting factors in the medication. This increased flow flushes out the accumulated lactic acid and begins the repair process of the micro-tears right away. Acetominophen is not as effective as the other medications, because it doesn't have the same blood thinning properties.

Tendinitis or fencer's elbow is a broad name given to any one of several injuries that can occur to the front arm near the elbow. Both the extensor muscle, which attaches to the outside bone of the elbow, and the tendons may be involved. Tendinitis itself is an inflammation in the tendon, a strong, stretchy band of tissue that attaches to a bone. This can occur near any joint, but the most typical location for tendinitis is in the forearm near the elbow of the weapon-arm — the fencing equivalent of tennis elbow. This happens because of several factors — repeated forearm stress from fencing against a heavy fencer who really bangs against your blade; clenching your weapon grip overly tightly, or not supinating the lead hand enough during arm extensions, are common possible causes. Tendinitis feels like a hot, sore sensation that doesn't improve with massage (like a cramp might). It feels worse after a workout and gets better with rest.

The first step in treating tendinitis is to rest the joints and muscles. Take a couple of weeks off from blade work, but keep the foot work going. At the same time, practice the following stretching exercise: Sit near a table or flat work surface, such as a dining table. Place your affected arm on the table, palm down, and dangle your hand over the edge. Keeping your forearm flat on the surface, raise your hand up and pull it backwards toward your body for a slow count of five. Let your fingers curl naturally. Then gently relax your hand and let it dangle again. Repeat this simple exercise three times, three or four sets daily, spread out over the day. It will only take a few minutes each time. If this exercise increases the amount of pain you feel, discontinue practice and see a physician.

After you've noticed improvement in your symptoms, you can add a small weight (1 pound or less) to the exercise, lifting gently and slowly, while keeping your forearm on the flat surface.

This particular simple exercise works by stretching and strengthening the muscle and tendon tissues and aligning the tendon into correct position. We've seen it work even on fencer's elbow of several year's duration.

Anyone who fences for several months will begin to notice *bruises*, most often from your opponent's blade impact. I get some of my nicest, bluest quarter-sized ones on my right upper arm, but women fencers also can be hit soundly on the breast, chest, shoulder, back and abdomen. The forward thigh also receives its share of spots. Personally, I consider these temporary injuries as clear signs of my participation in this exciting sport — and a good indicator of what areas I need to work harder to protect!

Bruises can be minimized by wearing sufficient padding and by making sure you get plenty of vitamin C by eating fresh fruits and vegetables.

Painful bruises respond to comfrey, a medicinal herb — but for best effect, you must apply the comfrey within minutes of receiving the bruise.

Blisters are also fairly common during the heat of a tournament. Typical locations are the heels, fingers of the weapon hand, and occasionally on the top of the foot. A blister, which is an area of raised skin with a small amount of clear fluid underneath it, results from repeated wearing against the skin surface. Sometimes you won't notice you're developing one until it breaks, leaving a damp spot on your sock or glove and a little sore spot where the wear occurred.

A self-sticking bandage applied before the blister

breaks is your best treatment. If it has already broken, wash with clean water and soap (antibacterial soap is excellent for this), cover with a little antibiotic gel or petroleum jelly, and finish with a self-stick bandage to protect from further wear. When the spot won't get further wear, remove the bandage and let it air dry. Occasional application of petroleum jelly will prevent it from getting too crusty. If a blister gets very red, weeps anything but clear fluid (such as a green or white discharge), has a red line extending away from it, or makes you feel feverish, please see your physician right away.

Somewhat less frequently than the injuries we've already discussed, but one that does occasionally happen, is *laceration*. A laceration is any kind of scratch or scrape that might happen when you are fencing – from a self-inflicted scratch off of a piece of metal sticking out of your mask to a scrape injury from a broken blade. There may be a little blood loss, similar to what might happen if you caught yourself on a rose-thorn. Treat this by washing in warm water with soap, pat dry, and apply antibiotic ointment. As with blisters, if any redness, swelling, serious pain, red lines or weeping occurs, please see your doctor right away.

Muscle cramps — an involuntary tightening of large muscles, typically in the lower leg, to the point of temporary pain — will affect almost everyone from time to time. They are not unique to fencing, but they sure can hurt!

Usually, the presence of leg cramps tells us something about how your entire body is processing fluids — you are probably a little bit dehydrated. So, the first treatment for persistent muscle cramps is simple: drink more water. If you don't like tap water, go ahead and get a good quality mineral water or spring water. If the weather is warm, a good 64 ounces daily will be very appreciated by your sore muscles!

Next, we consider the balance between sodium and potassium in your system – the electrolytes that are vital

Comfrey is an attractive tropical-looking plant with large leaves that can reach two feet in length. The leaves and stems have a bristly set of minute spines on them. The plant produces small lavender or white non-fragrant bell-like flowers on a central stem. Both the mucilaginous juice from the large root and leaves can be used to treat a bruise — the plant contains allatoin, an agent that increases the rate of cell repair.

Comfrey will grow easily anywhere in the United States when it has sufficient water and has been studied extensively in Great Britain for its potential as a green manure and livestock feed. Dried, ground leaves can be found in nearly any health food store in the world. Ancient Romans knew of its healing abilities and called it knitbone for its effects on broken limbs. The most amazing thing about comfrey, as a salve or tincture or even daubing with fresh leaves, is that the pain of a bruise is relieved almost instantly — and if used immediately after receiving the bruise, it will prevent the purple spot from appearing!

To prepare a comfrey salve, place one large handful of dried leaves or 4 or 5 fresh torn up leaves into 1 cup of olive oil. Simmer this until the vegetable matter is dark and deeply cooked, and the oil has taken on a green color from the plants. Strain the oil through a sieve and dispose of the cooked leaves. Place the oil in a heat-resistant jar (a mason-type canning jar is perfect) and add a quarter-sized piece of beeswax or paraffin while the oil is still hot. As the wax melts, stir gently with a spoon to distribute it. Let the mixture cool. If it is too runny, reheat it and add another quarter-size piece of wax — continue until it reaches a texture you like. If it was too firm, reheat and add several tablespoons of fresh olive oil to thin the mix a little. This salve will stain almost anything it touches!

Comfrey tincture is made by taking ½ cup of good quality vodka and steeping 4-5 crushed mashed leaves in it until the vodka turns a clear green color. This may take a week or longer. Strain out the leaves, save the alcohol in a small bottle — perhaps with a squeeze-dropper attached — and apply to bruises by dropfuls when needed. The green coloring may stain white clothing, but usually will come out in the wash.

to proper functioning of your muscles. If you have been sweating a good deal, you have lost these electrolytes along with the fluid sweat, and you need to replace them through the food you eat and liquids you drink. A daily multivitamin that contains potassium gluconate in the amount of 99 mg (milligrams) will often provide relief from muscle cramps — or a separate potassium pill daily will do the trick. Keep in mind here that more isn't necessarily better. A little extra potassium can help muscle function. Some health-conscious individuals, though, can go overboard with the idea and take much more of these supplements than their bodies require. A lot of extra potassium can interfere with normal function of all your muscles, including your heart. Be sensible.

In the same way, magnesium malate, magnesium asparate, or magnesium citrate, a chelated magnesium supplement, can improve overall cellular metabolism[1] and generally boost an individual's physical performance over time. Magnesium malate is a little harder to locate than magnesium combined with other supplements, but it is worth the extra effort.

Magnesium has other benefits for the woman fencer. Magnesium deficiencies have been implicated in migraines, pre-menstrual syndrome (PMS), allergies, abnormal blood fats, asthma, chronic bronchitis, diabetes, headaches, fluid retention, seizures, anxiety and panic reactions, heart disorders, high blood pressure, and the diseases of aging (such as dementia and senility).[2] Some researchers even believe that the notorious Syndrome X actually originates in a low cellular level of magnesium, which results in insulin overproduction and a host of health problems of the long term.

Most Americans do not consume even the recommended daily level (RDA) of magnesium, which can be enjoyed by eating more dark leafy green vegetables, nuts and seeds. Interestingly, our modern over-focus on calcium supplements might actually worsen the magnesium situation. Taking high levels of calcium can *deplete* our internal levels of magnesium since these two minerals must work hand-in-hand to produce their benefits. If you take too much calcium, you'll simply use up all the available magnesium trying to incorporate calcium, which leaves insufficient magnesium floating around your system to do the magnesium's share of the work. Ideally, your calcium and magnesium intake should balance one-to-one.

A daily dose of 300-400 mg of magnesium malate, aspartate or citrate will provide sufficient supplement for most Americans. An excess of magnesium in supplement form has one prominent side-effect: loose stools or diarrhea — the basis of the old time remedy of using epsom salts (crystallized magnesium) as a laxative! If you find this effect, take half as much magnesium supplement or back off the daily amount until the diarrhea ends.

Rare and Very Rare Injuries

This information is also from Eric D. Zemper, PhD and Peter Harmer, PhD, "Fencing" in Epidemiology of Sports Injuries, edited by D. Caine, C. Caine, K. Lindner. Published by Human Kinetics, Champaign, IL, 1996, pages 189-192.

Just like any sport people engage in, fencing has had a handful of more serious injuries attributed to it through the years. In fencing, there have been only seven deaths since 1937 in the entire sport in the world. All of these were elite or Olympic-level fencers. All were male. Since the introduction of the orthopedic or pistol grip, the only fatalities have been from pistol grip weapons — this is one of the many reasons we discourage using them. Not to make light of these sad occasions, it is still remarkable that a sport that originated in a killing art has had as few fatal accidents as it has.

Other rare injuries include cartilage tears, fractures, punctures, stress fractures, and subluxations. In almost 30 years of fencing, I have never seen a single instance of any of these — among tens of thousands of students fencing for hundreds of thousands of hours. We always advocate being conscious of your own body's mechanics, state of tiredness or alertness, and having the sensibility to not push yourself beyond your physical limitations — if you listen to your body, you won't hurt yourself.

Physical Issues Unique to the Woman Fencer

Not surprisingly, most of the uniquely female difficulties in fencing are involved with reproductive issues and related factors. Male fencers can fence year-round, year-in and year-out, from the time they first pick up the blade in their youth until they lay it down in old age. Nothing, except for major hospitalizations, needs to ever interfere with a good day's fencing.

A woman, on the other hand, blessed with the gift of generating new life, can easily be sidelined for 9-12 months during the gestation of each child. She can also be so uncomfortable with cramps or bloating every month for 35 or 40 years that she can't fence one week out of every four, can be run down from bad dieting behavior that she's too exhausted to fence, or can even fence so much that she begins a literal destruction of her own muscle and bone tissues. We're going to look at each of these in turn.

Pregnancy

Congratulations! You have become part of the river of life, giving your energy, your body, and a big part of your time over to the creation of a new human being! This is a heroic effort in many ways and deserves to be one of the best times of your life.

The physiological changes of pregnancy can produce a high feeling in some women, or a maternal drive that helps you organize your home, or an increase in intuition, or a feeling of continual tiredness. The hormonal changes can make you feel highly emotional and volatile, insecure, or filled with love for all of humanity. Physically, your breasts enlarge and fill with milk, your belly becomes your most-prominent feature, your weight will change (most often a significant increase), and your bladder becomes so compressed by the growing baby that you'll think it has shrunk to the size of a thimble.

Where is fencing in this astonishing series of changes? Realistically, it is on the sidelines. As the physical changes of pregnancy progress, those large breasts become exquisitely tender; a single light foil touch can be the source of astonishing pain. That growing belly throws your balance off — you might find yourself unusually clumsy at some point during the pregnancy, as your inner-ear struggles to maintain you upright against a shifting center of gravity. As the ligaments in your pelvis soften in preparation for childbirth, your lunges will be gawky and uncoordinated; for the first time, you may fall when you try to lunge. Other fencers will look at your burgeoning target area and hold back for fear of damaging the baby. Your fencing uniform will no longer fit.

What's left after that? A surprising amount of fencing can still be open to you. You can easily participate as both a judge and director — following the actions of a bout and observing (and learning from) the skills and techniques of other fencers. You can also take hand lessons from your maestro — working on parries, ripostes, complex counterattacks that do not require a lunge, and finessing your point control. Pregnancy is an ideal time to read about fencing history, techniques, theory and philosophy (see the resources at the back of the book); in nine months you'd be quite well-educated! Fencing movies can be enjoyed over and over: *The Princess Bride*, *By the Sword*, *The Mask of Zorro*, *The Man in the Iron Mask*, and *Cutthroat Island* are all available on video and provide the chance to enjoy cinematic fencing set in engaging story-lines. Bouting, however, should be avoided — along with any aspect of fencing in which you could be struck by an opponent's blade.

Light exercises — walking, lifting easy weights, swimming, stair-stepping, rowing, yoga, and so forth — will continue to be excellent options. You will feel better during your pregnancy if you can continue to keep active, and light exercise will make both the childbirth and post-pregnancy weight loss much easier.

Eating Disorders

It is fairly well accepted that people with the well-known eating disorders, anorexia nervosa (a refusal to eat, even when starving, with weight loss to life-threatening levels) and bulimia (binge-eating followed by vomiting or taking laxatives) are not merely trying to look like a magazine model. Women, and the few men afflicted with these disorders, simply cannot picture themselves as they are. They continue to imagine that they are unbearably fat, even when they reach skeletal proportions. Examples of women who have starved themselves to death — even while they believed they were profoundly obese date back to 1689[3], when the condition was called nervous consumption.

Women athletes in many sports — notably running, dancing, and gymnastics — are encouraged by trainers and public opinion to keep their weight down. And, spurred on by their own desire to both please their trainers and to win at their sport, women competitors will sometimes go to dangerous extremes to lose weight. For some women, this turns into anorexic or bulemic behaviors — starving, using laxatives and diuretics, followed by a period of crazed overeating, followed by further starvation. This cycle becomes self-repeating and can result in tooth loss, muscle and bone loss, and more serious complications including damage to the brain and other organs, and eventual premature death. Women who engage in these behaviors rarely think that they are actually endangering themselves. Often, this starving action feels instead like a form of control over difficult circumstances. Women, even successful athletes, who find themselves starving and binging, need help — professional help from a therapist or a physician. The earlier this behavior is treated, the better chance there will be for a return to healthy eating and self-image.

Fortunately, women fencers are much less likely than women in other sports to begin the starve/binge/starve cycle. Part of this comes from the fact that fencing doesn't require a diminutive, thin, lightweight competitor in order to produce wins. Fencing calls for cleverness, strategy, and rapid responses. Women of any weight or build can learn these attributes.

Fencing itself will refine and strengthen muscles throughout the body causing an overall loss of inches in all the important places (hips, thighs, and waist). Interestingly, a woman may find that while she looks and feels thinner and healthier, she doesn't lose much weight. This is because she has developed more muscles as she exercises, and muscles weigh more than fat does. If you are interested in weight loss, remember that it's not what the scales says that counts — it's how you feel and perform that matter.

A frustration for the full figured woman fencer continues to be the choices of jackets and assorted gear. Unlike the realistic clothing and fashion industries, who have realized that all women are not size 8, the companies that make fencing jackets and pants still remain unenlightened. Athletic women who are larger than size 16 may find they must use men's jackets and pants (it's apparently normal for men to reach larger sizes!) – and, even then, some sewing skills may be required to adjust for breasts and smaller shoulders. This is a field that is ripe for an entrepreneurial spirit, who could make garments for larger women fencers – and make a pretty decent income at the same time!

Over-exercising

Allied with the eating disorders, specifically with anorexia, is the over-exercise problem. This doesn't apply only to fencing, of course, but to any sport or physical activity taken to an extreme. In anorexia and occasionally bulimia, the sufferer — as part of the determination to lose weight — will begin a rigorous exercise program. Sometimes, this can become a prodigious effort, spending hours on stairmasters or weight machines or repeating footwork, trying to burn off the excess calories she mistakenly believes she had eaten.

This kind of exertion depletes both fat and muscle — tissues simply cannot replace themselves rapidly enough to keep the body at equilibrium. Remember, good exercise will build and strengthen muscle. Excess or too little exercise will tear them down.

How do you know if you are exercising too much, too little, or just enough? Over-exercise is characterized by compulsion — the constant, unpleasant inner pressure to repeatedly do something, even when it hurts, takes up too much time, or makes you feel unwell.

That last portion, *makes you feel unwell,* is a critical factor in over-exercising — excessive workouts make you feel tired, fatigued, exhausted, sore, and weak. Not just the day following the workout, but for days at a stretch. It's normal for muscles to feel a little sore and for you to feel a little tired the day after a healthy workout — but if that soreness and exhaustion extends longer, you are simply not letting your muscles recover from the work they've had to do. Exercising when you are already tired does NOT build muscles or improve your coordination — it breaks down tissues and leaves you with less ability than before.

If you find yourself aware of a pushing need to fence or engage in workouts even when you're already tired and achy, there may be other issues in your life that need to be resolved — fencing is becoming a dodge instead of a joy.

Previously, we've discussed micro-tears that occur in muscle under extreme use. Actually, even ordinary use of muscles — walking around, mowing the lawn, washing dishes, stretching, painless activities of daily life — all speed breakdown of minute muscle tissues. Fortunately, our bodies are designed to absorb torn and broken cells and to replace them at remarkable rates — sore muscles feel better after a few days' rest because they've had a chance to regenerate new tissues.

In the same way, bone cells are made and layered onto your current bone structure. Good, healthy levels of exercise actually increase your bone strength by building new bone cells and cementing them onto your existing bones. Excessive exercise — overdoing it continuously — doesn't let your body rest.

It is during rest that the repair and reconstruction goes on. No rest = no new bone building = bone loss.

Constantly over-exercising can be intensely damaging to your bones. Bone damage shows up as stress factures. Tiny breaks in major bone (such as the femur head, the joint that attaches your leg to your hip) or in ankles or wrists are fairly clear signs that you haven't allowed your body to recover from earlier exercise. Unfortunately, many women runners experience this type of fracture, an indicator that too much exercise and not enough rest has been going on. Don't let the presence of a coach or team advisor derail you from listening to your own body, either. Coaches can sometimes get lost in their own ambitions and inspirations and push athletes beyond safety. No medal, no goal, no sports award is worth sacrificing your health over. The glory lasts for a few moments; your health is for the rest of your life.

Amenorrhea

Over-exercising has a further component that is connected to generalized bone loss thru lack of rest and rebuilding. It is bone loss that occurs when the female athlete stops menstruating.

A brief detour helps explain this difficulty. Our monthly menses are more than a source of irritation — they are the physiological preparation to support another human life. Your womb, or uterus, builds up a blood-rich lining that can act as a growing medium for a newly implanted fetal baby, another person in the act of growing in your body.

The entire month-long process begins with a surge in various hormones that promote physical changes — we cycle through moods, through food desires, through physical temperatures, and through states of mind at the same time. Some women feel these changes more sharply than others, and as the uterine lining begins to deteriorate when no fertile egg implants, these women experience the familiar pre-menstrual syndrome (PMS).

It is during the pre-menstrual phase, when PMS is at its peak, when many women notice that they are extra irritable, feel bloated, retain fluids, crave certain foods (chocolate is common), become forgetful, moody, or easily confused, and feel particularly clumsy. In spite of how unpleasant this can be, it is relatively normal. (The females of other species, such as horses and pigs, also go through similar monthly cycles, with similar moody ups-and-downs.) It is only when PMS becomes extreme, interfering with daily life, disrupting relationships, causing you to make destructive decisions, that the situation requires treatment.

Some women find that they are able to fence with greater skill, clarity, and speed during the first two days of their menstrual period. The hormonal changes make them feel clearer-headed and able to move better. Other women feel sluggish and tired. Your own individual response is your best guide. If you feel better, fence! If you feel worse, relax and enjoy a rest!

After the menses begin, your body sheds the uterine lining during the course of about five to seven days — you have your monthly period. The blood loss associated with this phase depletes your body's supply slightly, about a cup of blood or less — half as much as you'd give up when donating blood. Iron is actually the component of the blood that is responsible for the red coloration, the *heme* in hemoglobin. Not too many years ago, medicine believed that this loss of iron in the blood left women temporarily weakened and anemic. Today, the newest conception of the iron loss associated with the menstrual flow is that is helps protect women against heart disease — which partially explains why women's rate of heart attacks increases after menopause to match that of men — no more beneficial iron loss associated with monthly periods. Other findings suggest that women who take oral contraceptives (birth control pills) have a three or four times higher risk for developing heart disease than those who have never taken the pills — possibly because these women have shorter, lighter menstrual flows and a higher level of stored iron.

In trying to understand the relationship of iron-level to cardiovascular disease, there are other pieces of the puzzle. It's known that people who smoke have a higher blood iron level — it carries the oxygen that we need in our tissues. They also have a higher heart disease rate than people who have never smoked. Smokers, clearly, would need greater oxygen-carrying capacity, since the act of smoking itself depletes oxygen from the lungs — replacing it with carbon monoxide, dioxide, and smoke particles! The body simply becomes more efficient at transporting a lessened amount of oxygen, by making more heme iron.

Eades and Eades[4] wondered why the long course of human development would lead to a condition in which excess iron would become a potential health problem. On one hand, it seems like excess iron should be quite beneficial — clearly there are physical mechanisms in place to build up the iron level, such as fast blood cell generation following a bleeding injury, and the fact that our bodies have no mechanism for excreting excesses. On the surface, it seems as though "the more iron the better" would be the rule; but it isn't. A little circulating iron is both vital and beneficial, but too much creates serious problems. Iron, in too steep a concentration, has

PMS remedies: Many herbal preparations and natural methods have been used over the years to deal with the symptoms of PMS. Here's a list of what some women have said worked for them:

1. reduce caffeine
2. reduce sugar/carbohydrate consumption
3. herbal teas including real red raspberry leaf, or chickweed, or cranberry, or squaw root, or feverfew
4. evening primrose oil caplets
5. vitamin B6
6. magnesium malate, citrate, or aspartate
7. plan to relax and take it easy for a few days
8. long quiet walks on nature trails
9. meditate or pray
10. warm or hot packs placed on the lower abdomen
11. pamper yourself: bubble bath and expensive cologne
12. some women report that making love relieves both cramps and stress at this time!

even been known to poison children who consume iron pills that look like candy.

The realization occurred to the Eades quite suddenly: A principal difference between today's civilized lifestyle and the way our ancestors have lived for millennia — and a possible reason why primitive people today have a much lower rate of heart disease than Westerners —is parasites.

All through human history, people and their companions — intestinal worms, lice, fleas, bedbugs, various types of blood-sucking insects — have coexisted in an apparently mutually-adapted or symbiotic relationship. The parasites deplete blood by attaching to the intestines and either drawing it off directly or by absorbing nutrients from the passing food so that the host human doesn't get as rich a diet. Lice and other undesirables draw blood away through the skin surface. Either way, the ancient and primitive human had a constantly depleted iron level through most of his or her life (parasites only became a problem when the host was weakened by disease or injury), and was in a constant state of attempting to replenish and hold onto that iron by generating new blood cells. The rate of iron generation came to match the amount the parasites were withdrawing. Meantime, we enlightened modern parasite-free humans build up iron to health-threatening levels when we don't lose blood routinely.

Consider yourself lucky that you shed blood on a monthly basis, because that protects you from the effects of excess circulating iron! Some authorities believe that post-menopausal women — and healthy adult men of any age, too — can reduce their risk of heart disease by giving blood once every two months. This could reduce their iron level sufficiently to prevent the damage excess heme iron can cause.

Menstruation isn't only a physiological preparation for pregnancy, and a way of depleting excess iron stores. For the female athlete its regular occurance is also an excellent indicator of general health. Regular menses demonstrate that your body fat level — that vital component of nerves and brain cells — is adequate. If your body fat level slips too low — as it will if you starve yourself, or if you exercise too much — you will simply stop menstruating. For many years, women's coaches and physicians insisted that the cessation of menstruation wouldn't be harmful. Today, however, physicians insist that amenorrhea is NOT a benign condition.

The lack of menstrual periods, is also a clear indicator of something else: bone loss. Amenorrheic female athletes are the ones who show stress fractures and significant bone loss — sometimes so much bone loss that young women in their 20s and 30s have the weakened porous bones of 70- and 80-year-olds. No amount of oral calcium supplements will replace the important physiological benefits of maintaining your weight and body fat at an adequate level — a level that preserves your ability to menstruate.

Fencing in the second half of life

A good, hard workout is fun and beneficial; too many hard workouts that result in the loss of your periods also will cost you your bones and damage your cardiovascular system. Fortunately, the typical woman fencer is very sensible about her health and finds that eating reasonably, fencing enough to exercise and build muscles, and listening to her body's need for rest all produces the best results!

Menopause and Beyond

At some time between the age of 35 and about 55, most women pass through the natural stage of menopause — the permanent cessation of ovulation and menses. Menopause, like puberty, can be a time of emotional and physical turmoil: moodiness, hot flashes, changes in body shape and performance, a whole host of differences. In addition to the physical changes, many women also go through a midlife transition — where you begin to look back on the life you have made and come to understand that it is not as you expected it to be. You recognize that half your life is over. Has it been good enough? Fun enough? Worth the effort? Did it go in the right direction? What if you had made different decisions?

A woman in this phase of life begins to see new options, new opportunities. The children, who occupied so much of your middle years, have gone on to their own lives. Your spouse is competent in his work, or he is making a transition of his own into other employment, other directions. If you are single, or between partners, you begin to think about what it will be like in 10 years, in 15 years, in retirement. What decisions can you make *now* that will make the next 20 years better, more active, healthier, more enjoyable?

Fencing can be a part of the rest of your life. It can help make it active, healthy and enjoyable. As a mature woman, you will approach fencing with a recognition that you're not going to learn it all overnight. You'll be more willing than younger fencers to spend the time it takes to perfect your form and hone your skills. When you do begin bouting, you'll be conscious of your limits and be more willing to treat your body with respect. You won't be as fast, initially, as the young pups, but you'll gain speed and you will be a *lot* faster and more agile than many other women your age. And, if you wish, there are many, many opportunities to compete in fencing for veterans — women take home medals in foil, sabre, and épée well into their golden years.

Physically, the activity of fencing will keep joints supple, improve your balance, increase your cardiovascular capacity, and help prevent bone loss. Fencing is also a superb confidence builder for the mature woman, especially one who has spent her earlier years avoiding conflicts and disagreements — the bout situation gives you a way to respond to other points of view with strategy and composure!

Finally, the fencing salle is a place where your maturity is likely to garner respect. When you land a resounding touch on a younger opponent, watch for the change

in his or her expression — that is an image you will remember for a long time!

NOTES

1 Michael R. Eades, M.D. and Mary Dan Eades, M.D.,
   The Protein Power Lifeplan, p. 223.
2 Michael R. Eades, M.D. and Mary Dan Eades, M.D.,
   The Protein Power Lifeplan, p. 224-5.
3 Jerrold S. Maxmen and Nicholas G. Ward, *Essential
   Psychopathology and Its Treatment*, p. 332.
4 Michael R. Eades, M.D. and Mary Dan Eades, M.D.,
   The Protein Power Lifeplan, p. 173-204.

SECTION FOUR
HOW TO
FENCE

THE BASIC CONCEPTS

Now, we will talk about the process of fencing, the form and method, the *how to* and *how not to* of the game. This will be more of an overview, however, rather than an all-inclusive treatise. The goal of this chapter and the following two chapters, is to give you a feeling for fencing, a beginning exposure, a starting place upon which to build your skills. Actual lessons with a teacher, of course, are a must, as will be bouting with other fencers. Other reading materials will also help.

The information included here is pretty much the same for women as for men. The act of fencing, the mechanical game, is what it is, regardless of gender. So is the mental game. Fencing is very much a logical, common sense pursuit and therefore the bastion only of the intelligent individual, whoever that person — man or woman — might be.

Now, on with the lesson.

Fencing

As we have already noted elsewhere in this book, when we break it down to its basic concept, fencing, pure and simple, is the act of hitting your opponent with your weapon *and* not being hit yourself. Certainly, this is the goal we focus on when we take up fencing. Why else would anyone want to fence? The question is, how do we best accomplish this outcome?

The goal of fencing

The Goal of Fencing

But within the act of fencing itself we have a goal that overrides the act of simply hitting an opponent. We want more than anything else to hit without being hit ourselves. And herein lies the need for a process that will allow you to do this on a regular basis, a process that makes getting touches a controlled act rather than luck.

The Process of Fencing

The process of fencing is the method by which you move from point A (your weapon) to point B (your opponent's target area). It is the way in which you view yourself and your opponent, the way in which you interact, physically and mentally, with your opponent. How you embrace this process will determine the depth of your fencing game. Making your game a purely physical one will promote a superficiality that will keep it a one-note affair for as long as you fence. Blending mind and body will allow you to internalize your fencing game, giving you a rich and lasting skill.

The Weapons of Fencing

There are three weapons in the modern sport of fencing: the foil, the épée, and the sabre. Each possesses its own unique personality, its own methodology, its own mindset. To become truly proficient at any weapon, it is important for you to understand the purpose of that weapon, and where it falls in the scheme of fencing.

The Foil

We will start our discussion of weapons with the foil because it is traditionally the weapon fencers begin with. It is the teaching weapon of fencing. With a flat-tipped, flexible blade for safety, the foil is 44 inches long from point to pommel (the blade takes up 3 feet of that length) and weights 16 ounces.

The use of the foil — French, Italian, or pistol grip — is guided by conventions, or rules that demand a particular type of behavior from the fencer. These conventions are based on a common sense approach to sword combat, basically what you should be doing if the weapons you and your opponent were using had sharp blades. The foil may hit only with the point. The target area is the trunk of the body. The foil, more than anything else, teaches control and judgment on the fencing strip.

The Épée

The épée is the dueling sword of fencing. It descended from the rapier, the dueling weapon of the seventeenth century. It is the same length as the foil, but the blade is more rigid. The épée weights about 27 ounces. Like the foil, it is a point weapon; unlike the foil, it can hit anywhere on an opponent's body, just as in a real sword fight. Moreover, as in an actual duel, there are no conventions to guide you here. Only simple methodology guided by timing and discernment, prevent the épée fencer from being touched. In épée the idea is to hit first. The épée bout, therefore, should always be approached carefully, as though you were engaging in a real sword fight. And because you may be attempting to hit your opponent on something as narrow as his or her wrist, point control is of particular importance. Also, while a fencer's actions may be directed to a certain extent by strategy in épée, the épée is very much a weapon of the moment, an improvisational weapon. Being able to take advantage of momentary weaknesses that ar e here one second and gone the next is a vital skill and one of épée's greatest challenges.

The Sabre

The sabre is the third weapon of fencing. It evolved from the heavy military sabre of the nineteenth century. It is both shorter and lighter than either the foil or the épée. It is 42¼ inches long, the blade taking up 2 feet, 11⅛ of that length. In fencing's learning process, it is customarily the last weapon to be mastered because it is the most divergent in the way it is used. Like the foil, the sabre is a conventional weapon, that is, its usage is governed by a code of action. Unlike both the foil and the épée, the sabre may hit with either a thrust or a cut. This makes the mechanics of sabre considerably broader and flashier than anything encountered in foil or épée. The sabre target area is the body from the waste upward, including the head and arms.

Picking Your Weapon Grip

The sabre has one basic grip, but for both foil and épée you will have some choices to make when it comes to picking a weapon handle. The choice will affect your fencing future.

There are three distinctive types of grips for foil and épée: French, Italian, and pistol.

French

The French grip is my own personal favorite. It has a bend in the grip that fits into the bend of your hand. Its design promotes finger control of the weapon, which helps create a light, pliable game of finesse for the fencer.

Italian

The Italian grip promotes a strong but still maneuverable fencing game, reflecting the Italian school, which is a physically dominating style of fencing. To further enhance its application, the Italian grip is bound to the fencer's wrist with a leather or plastic strap.

Pistol

The pistol grip is by far the most popular type of grip used by fencers today. Sometimes called an *anatomical* or *orthopedic* grip, this type of handle comes in a number of styles. But they all have in common prongs around which the fencer wraps his or her fingers. Although the pistol grip is the dominant form of grip being used today, it does have problems. Chiefly, it causes the fencer to squeeze tightly, which both negates any opportunity for developing finger control and promotes a heavy, muscular approach to fencing. This also means a reduction in point control. Of course, many fencers like the strength they derive from pistol grips, hence their present popularity. When you come to fencing, you will doubtlessly be told more than once that pistol grips are a gift from the gods! I recommend to all my students that they stay far, far away from these items and instead learn the subtle intricacies of fencing.

Conventions

Now we need to stop a moment and talk about fencing conventions, perhaps *the* most misunderstood element of fencing. Conventions govern "right-of-way" in fencing. That is, who has the right to hit whom at any given moment on the fencing strip. Why have such rules? Many fencers argue that a real sword fight has no rules. Rules, they reason, are artificial, fake.

On one hand this is true. A real sword fight follows

no conventions. But, because of this, if you found yourself in such a dangerous situation, you'd better be sure you had control over what you were doing, or you'd probably be stuck painfully on the end of your opponent's blade. But how does one ever develop this kind of judgment?

You guessed it!

Conventions.

When we come to fencing, we bring our everyday people reactions of life. These are fine for walking and cooking and driving cars, but they get in the way on the fencing strip. Conventions possess a built-in common sense, a logic gleaned from centuries of sword fighting. They force us to adhere to a process that will produce the best effect possible, that is, *to hit one's opponent and not be hit in return.* A good idea, huh?

By following the rules of right-of-way, we learn that the best attack is one that creates a definite advantage over one's opponent through the use of distance, timing, and blade placement. We also learn that when we find ourselves at a disadvantage — when we are being menaced by a valid attack — we must defend ourselves, that is, parry. That is all conventions are really about: advantage and disadvantage.

So, beneath the surface of the statement that conventions are artificial or silly, we find that this is not so, that conventions are vital to learning the byplay of fencing. It is safe to say that without the aid of conventions, fencing would never be anything more than a hit-or-miss proposition, a game of chance, of accident.

FOIL

As I said, if you are smart, you will begin your fencing training with foil. Once upon a time, this would have been a given, a fact of fencing. But, today there are schools where you can pick the weapon you want to start with. Some teachers find no problem with this. So, I will just caution you: Beginning your fencing career with either the épée or sabre will more than likely instill traits into your game that will ruin you for any other weapon. The foil, on the other hand, teaches you all the foundational necessities of fencing: timing, distance, point control, strategy, judgment, balance, and self-discipline. These things, of course, translate well into épée and sabre. Think about it.

We will, by the way, be following the French school of fencing, which is my specialty.

Now, on to learning foil.

On Guard

We will start at the very beginning, learning the on guard position. It is the position of readiness, both offensively and defensively. It must be balanced and relaxed, because without these attributes, you will always be both unsteady and tense on the fencing strip.

Feet

How you position your feet will determine your success at maintaining balance. So it is very important, from

On guard (front view).

the start to be aware of what you are doing with your feet.

1. We start with the feet together, forming a right angle. The right foot, the lead foot, points straight ahead in the direction of your opponent. This puts the feet in a lined up, balanced position.
2. Now step forward with the right foot, keeping your heels lined up. Your feet should now be between 18 and 24 inches apart, depending on your height.
3. The feet must maintain this line-up for maximum balance.

Knees

The bent knee position is distinctive to the fencing stance, and is important in producing easy movement.

1. Bend both your knees equally so that that your weight is equally distributed on both legs. We call this "sitting down." Basically, it lowers your center of gravity, giving you maximum balance when you are on guard.
2. How deeply should you bend your knees? Not so much that it puts a strain on your muscles, not so little that you can't feel your center of gravity lowering.
3. By the way, never shift your weight from leg to leg. This will cause you to lean, which will definitely throw you off balance.

Gripping the Foil

Next, let's look at how you hold the foil — if you are holding a French foil, that is. How you grip it will either make it a highly maneuverable extension of your fingers or turn it into a lumbering club.

1. The French grip has a slight bend in it that fits into the bend of your sword hand. Also, by the way the grip is attached to the blade, the wide

On guard (side view)

part of the grip corresponds to the wide part of the blade.

2. You will be cradling the grip between your thumb and first finger pressing on either wide side of the grip.
3. Don't squeeze!
4. The last three fingers of your sword hand fold over the grip, holding it lightly in place.

Sword Arm Position

How you hold your sword arm will either promote a relaxed attitude or tire your arm out in a few minutes of fencing. Too straight of an arm will generate tension. Too much bend will constrict your movement. The correct position, however, will generate easy, unrestricted movement.

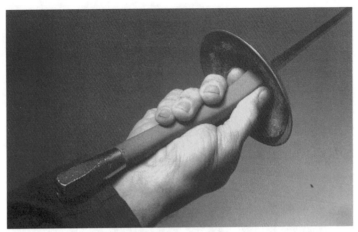

Holding the foil

1. Bend your sword arm so that your elbow points down to your right knee.
2. The sword arm should not be bent so much that that your upper arm is pressed close to your torso.
3. The sword arm should not be so straight that it is difficult to tell that it's bent (beginners often forget to keep their arm bent when on guard).

Sword Hand Position

Where you place your sword hand in relationship to your body will either overbalance or exaggerate what you do with your foil or lead to small precise blade movements.

1. When on guard, your sword hand should be held at chest level.
2. The foil should be held in partial supination (supination means palm up). This is done by placing your thumb in a "one o'clock" position. For instance, at twelve o'clock, the thumb would be straight up; one o'clock is just short of that).
3. This partially supinated sword hand position helps to keep your hand relaxed.

Foil Position

This must be viewed in conjunction with the sword hand.

1. The foil grip is held at chest level.
2. The point of your foil is held at your own eye level.
3. Place the foil blade in line, with your nose.

Free Arm Position

The free arm never touches the foil, but it does have a lot to do with whether or not the foil will be employed efficiently. When you are on guard, it acts as a counterbalance (it also has other functions with regard to the lunge, which we will be discussing presently).

1. The free arm is bent and held up and away from the body at about a 45-degree angle,
    which causes the body to angle toward one's opponent.
2. The upper part of the arm (nearest the shoulder) is held at shoulder height.
3. From the elbow, the arm is held straight up.
4. The free hand, pointing forward, is held loosely.

Free arm position

The Lines of the Body

In fencing, the body is divided up into four quarters, with each quarter representing a portion of the fencer's body. We call these quarters lines. The lines above the sword hand are called the high lines. Those below the sword hand are called the low lines. The lines closest to the chest are called the inside lines. Those closest to the back are the outside lines. That gives us a high inside line and a high outside line and a low inside line and a low outside line.

Moreover, each line has a corresponding number, which is further based on whether the sword hand is held in supination (palm up) or pronation (palm down). Because there are four quarters, that gives us four supinated positions and four pronated positions, or eight positions in all. The names for these positions are numbers, which are designated in Old French and Latin. In the language of fencing, they are prime, seconde, tierce, quarte, quinte, sixte, septime, and octave; in English, they are one, two, three, four, five, six, seven, and eight.

Prime, seconde, tierce, and quinte are pronated hand positions. Quarte, sixte, septime, and octave are supinated hand positions.

In the French school, we use mainly the supinated hand positions, because they tend to generate light, precise actions that emanate from the fingers. Pronated hand positions generally produce heavier actions that come from the shoulder. The latter are what the French school tries to avoid.

In the French school, by the way, 90 percent of what goes on in foil fencing takes place in the lines of quarte/four (the high inside line with the sword hand held in supination) and sixte/six (the high outside line with the sword hand held in supination).

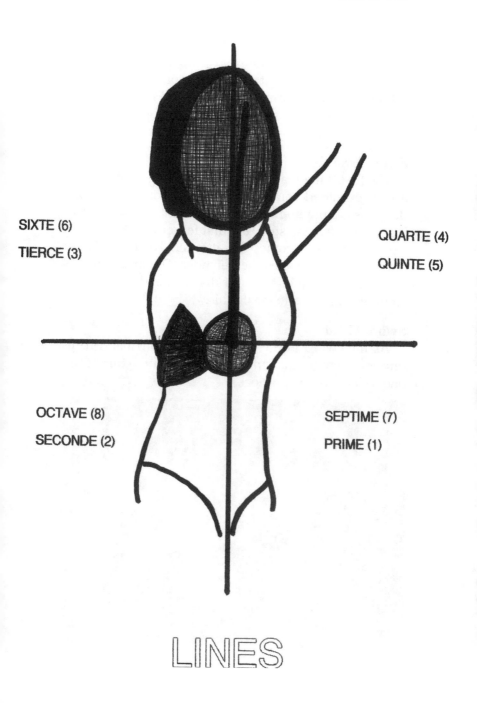

SIXTE (6)

TIERCE (3)

QUARTE (4)

QUINTE (5)

OCTAVE (8)

SECONDE (2)

SEPTIME (7)

PRIME (1)

LINES

The Lunge

The lunge is the action that propels your attack toward your opponent. It is made up of numerous body actions that, if performed correctly, will maximize your ability to deliver your point onto your opponent's target.

Sword Arm

The first thing that happens in the lunge is the sword arm is extended completely straight from your shoulder. This is a requirement of the conventions of foil fencing. On the fencing strip, the first fencer to extend his or her sword arm becomes the attacker. The other fencer automatically becomes the defender. The idea is to create an advantage in terms of distance and timing. The straight arm helps to create this.

Sword Hand

As the sword arm extends, your sword hand turns into complete supination (that is, your thumb turns from one o'clock to three o'clock).

The lunge

The free arm drops on the lunge

Foil Blade

Your foil blade should now be parallel to the ground.

Rear Leg

After the sword arm has been extended, the forward movement of the lunge may begin. This is created by the rear leg straightening — actually being snapped straight — which propels the fencer forward in an accelerating push. This provides the lunge with the velocity it needs to get past the opposing fencer's defenses.

Front Foot

As the back leg straightens, the front foot is lifted off the ground, which propels the body forward. This resembles a stepping action, but the entire thrust of the lunge comes from the back leg. The front foot is merely your "landing gear."

Free Arm

At the same movement that the back leg is straightening, the free arm is thrown back quickly until it is straight. This adds to the forward thrust and also promotes balance in the lunge.

Front Foot/Front Knee

Once you have reached the full potential of your lunge in terms of distance, your front foot is set down heel first. At the same moment, your front knee is pushed forward until it is directly over your front ankle.

The Lunge Completed

The lunge is now complete.

Practicing the Lunge

The lunge you practice should be comfortable and consistent, and not necessarily based on covering a long distance. Rather it should allow you mobility and the ability to recover easily from your extended position if necessary.

Also, remember the sword arm is always straight before you start moving forward with the actual lunge. This is a requirement of foil fencing!

The Recovery

After the lunge has been completed, the recovery back into the on guard position is produced by pushing off

A successful attack

from the front foot and pulling the free arm back quickly into its previous position. When you are back fully in the on guard position, it should look exactly as it did before you lunged.

Simple Attacks

The definition of a simple attack is an attack made up entirely of timing and speed where you are trying to hit your opponent before a defensive move can be launched. There are four simple attacks:

The Straight Hit

The first simple attack is the straight hit. It is produced simply by extending your sword arm straight in the line you are on guard in and lunging.

Disengage/Degagé

The second and most popular simple attack is the disengage (or in French the degagé). It is produced by passing your blade from one line to an opposite line, passing beneath your opponent's blade. The sword arm extends as your blade passes to the other line. This is followed instantly by a lunge.

Coulé

The third simple attack is the coulé (which in French means "running"). It is an attack that glides along your opponent's blade in the same line you are on guard in. As your blade travels down your opponent's blade, your sword arm extends until it is completely straight. Once this is established, you lunge.

Coupé

The final simple attack is the coupé (meaning "cut over"). It is an attack that passes from one line to the opposite line passing over the top of your opponent's blade. It is done by pulling the forearm back just enough so that your foil blade clears the top of your opponent's blade. Once this happens, your blade point is dropped into the other line, and your sword arm is extended straight. This action should be done in a single flowing motion. Once your point is down, and your arm is straight, you may lunge.

Using Simple Attacks

These are our simple attacks. Not one is any better or worse than the others. Each is just a different way of presenting your blade for a possible touch. Each has a slightly different timing; each produces a slightly different visual effect. By mixing them up sufficiently well, you will be doing your best to keep your opponent off guard.

The Parry

The definition of a parry is that it is an action that knocks or pushes your opponent's attacking blade defensively. That is, your opponent is attacking you, and you are keeping the advancing blade from touching you.

Lateral and Counter Parries

There are two types of parries: lateral parries and counter parries. Lateral parries move back-and-forth in a straight line. Counter parries go around in a circle.

Supination

In the French school, almost all the parries you will do will be made in partial supination (with your sword thumb at one o'clock).

Quarte and Sixte

The lateral parries of quarte and sixte cover those lines respectively. Lateral parries stop an attack in the line into which the attack has been made.

Contre de Quarte and Contre de Sixte

The counter parries of countre de quarte (which travels counter clockwise) and countre de sixte (which travels clockwise) do the opposite of lateral parries, contre

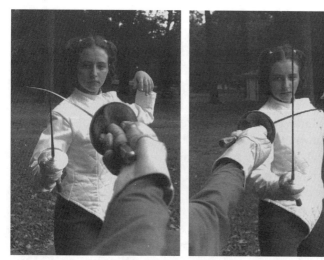

Parrying an attack in the line   *Parrying an attack in the line*
of sixte (high-outside line)   *of quarte (high-inside line)*

de quarte defending the sixte line and countre de sixte defending the quarte line. Basically, these parries follow the attacking blade around and return it to the line from which the attack originated.

Opposition and Detached Parries

Parries may be made as parries of opposition or as detached parries. A parry of opposition pushes the attacking blade out of the way. The detached parry, also called a beat or tec parry, uses the spring inherent in both blades to displace the attacking blade. With a detached parry, the parry is created by snapping the blade from the fingers. This produces firm contact that will easily knock your opponent's blade aside without extended contact. This allows for an easy transition to the producing a counterattack. The detached parry is the preferred form of defense in the French school.

Riposte

The riposte is the counterattack following a successful parry. It is sometimes called the "echo of the parry," because it should follow the parry without hesitation.

When the parrying blade recoils off (detaches from) the deflected attacking blade, the first thing that happens is the sword hand turns into complete supination (the thumb, again, turns from one o'clock to three o'clock). This both controls the strong recoil and drops your blade point toward your opponent, placing it in line automatically with the target area. This simple mechanical action is how point control is achieved. Not through force or will power. Just turning the hand up off that recoil of the parry is all you need!

Once the point is in line with your opponent's chest, you merely extend your sword arm as far as you need to make a touch. If you need to extend your arm completely straight, do so. If you need only a partial extension, go with that. Remember, your opponent, as the initial attacker, will determine your maneuvering distance, and you must adjust your riposte to fit that reality.

It is also important to remember to make the riposte immediately following your parry. Hesitation will allow your opponent to continue with their attack (which, when done in the same line, is called a remise; and, in the opposite line, a redoublement).

Composed Attacks

Composed attacks (also called composite and complex attacks) are where fencing really takes on the appearance of chess.

The definition of a composed attack is an attack that is made up first of a feint of an attack, followed immediately by a deception of your opponent's subsequent parry. What does this mean?

Feint

The feint is a pretend attack. This feint — and it may be a feint of any attack, such as a feint of disengage, for instance — is made as a threat, an action to draw your

Practicing the feint (photo by Anita Evangelista)

opponent into making a parry. It has to look like a real offensive action. The only difference is that there is no lunge. If you lunge, the action is no longer a feint but a full-fledged attack. Again, the feint is made only to draw a defensive response out of your opponent. The ultimate purpose of this feint is to draw your opponent's blade in one direction or another, so it will not be where you actually want to make your touch. In effect, you are trying to create a hole in your opponent's defense. That is why you make a feint. Therefore the feint must look like what it's not. If it looks like what it is, a fake action, your opponent will not be impressed and will not make a parry.

Deception

Once your opponent responses to your threatening feint with a parry, your job is to deceive (evade/dodge) that parry. By doing so, you have indeed penetrated your opponent's defense. Again, this latter move is totally reliant on the quality of your feint. A poor feint will not draw a parry, which means you will have nothing to deceive.

Lunge

Once you have cleared your opponent's parry, you may lunge.

One-Two and Doublé

We have two basic composed attacks: the one-two and the doublé (pronounced: du-blay).

The one-two is made up of a feint of disengage and a decepton of one lateral parry. Basically, the feint draws a lateral parry, which is then evaded by dropping your own blade beneath it and putting your weapon back into the line in which you began your attack. Then, you lunge.

The doublé is made up of a feint of disengage and a deception of one counter parry. In this case, the feint of disengage elicits a counter parry, which is evaded by directing your blade movement in the same direction that the parry is traveling, thereby outrunning the parry. The action could be described as a small circle (deception) within a large circle (parry).

Which Parry?

So, how do you happen to figure out which parry — lateral or counter — that your opponent will be using? You make feints, and you watch the reactions the feints produce. Simply put, your opponent will show you how they will respond. This is by no means foolproof. But it will give you good indications on how to base your composed attacks.

Variations

Along with the two basic composed attacks, we may produce composed attacks by combining one simple attack with another simple attack (such as a coulé-disengage or a disengage-coupé), simple attacks with composed attacks (such as a doublé-coupé or a coulé-one-two), or by joining composed attacks together (such as a one-two-doublé or a doublé-one-two). Combinations, therefore, are virtually unlimited. It would be possible to do a coule-doublé-one-two-coupé-disengage-coupé-disengage. It's not likely you would normally get this complex with an attack, but it is possible.

Strategy

Foil, fenced in the most intelligent way possible, is very much like a game of chess. It is a game of moves and counter moves. But how you frame those moves will be based entirely on how your opponent defends herself. Your strategy will be colored by whether your opponent is reactive or thoughtful, whether their actions are light or heavy, whether they are aggressive or timid, whether they have good distance or poor. You must have a mental connection to your opponent and mold your actions on what you observe. And because every fencer will be a little bit different than all the others you meet, setting up appropriate strategies will be one of your biggest challenges on the fencing strip. If you learn to do it well, though, it will be one of the most satisfying aspects of your fencing.

ÉPÉE AND SABRE

Because this book is basically an introduction to fencing, we will not go into any detail on either the épée or sabre, which are advanced fencing weapons. But we will touch on them, simply to provide the reader with a glimpse into their operation.

Women have probably fenced with épées and sabres for as long as women have been sport fencing, but official sanctions for women to fence these weapons are a relatively recent happening. Today, women in the U.S. have nationally ranked contests in épée and sabre.

Épée

In the arsenal of fencing weapons, the épée is the second weapon for you to think about learning. The épée is the dueling sword of fencing and should always be approached with this concept in mind. This means a careful and deliberate mindset, as though you were fighting with sharp-bladed weapons. If you come to épée with this outlook, you will infuse your game with a personality making it unique from the other two weapons.

The épée, like the foil, is a point weapon. Unlike the foil, the target area in épée is the entire body, as it would be in a real fight. Also, unlike foil, there are no rules, or conventions, that govern the way the épée must be employed. With épée, the idea is to hit first — period.

The épée

While the épée has its strategies, it is also very much a weapon of the moment, a spontaneous, improvisational weapon. To be able to take advantage of momentary flaws in your opponent's offense or defense is the hallmark of the expert épéeist. This requires excellent timing and point control, in my opinion the two most important attributes an épéeist can acquire. A sound sense of distance is also very important.

You can take lessons to learn specific épée moves from your teacher, but the best way to learn to fence épée is to fence épée. On-the-job training.

On Guard

The on guard position for épée is similar to foil, except for one major difference: the sword arm is held nearly straight, with the point of the weapon position slightly below the level of the sword hand. This does two things: first, it keeps one's point in a menacing position with regard to an opposing fencer; and, second, it protects the hand and forearm from immediate attack.

Supination/Pronation

The sword hand may be held in either pronation or

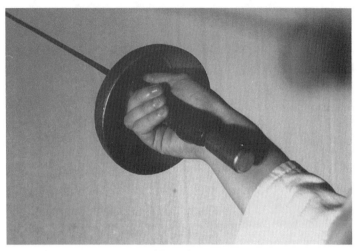

Holding the épée

supination, depending on whether you plan on attacking above (supination) or below (pronation) your opponent's guard.

Offense

Épée offense should be approached with much deliberation. To not be hit is better than forcing a double touch. If you're not going to take épée fencing in the spirit in which it was created — as practice for dueling — why bother with it?

Attacks should be accomplished with the idea of defensive offence. This means, no matter what attack you do, or what part of your opponent's body you attempt to hit, your actions should not leave you open to stop or time thrusts. Basically, even when attacking, your body parts should be protected by your actions.

Defense

Defense should be accomplished, as much as possible, with the notion of offensive defense. This means, that you should not go completely defensive if you can help it. This will leave you open to counterattacks. By keeping your épée point in line and parrying as much as possible with your hand guard, you keep your opponent in continuous peril.

Strategy

Although you may hit your opponent anywhere from head to foot, the obvious best choice for a touch is the body part closest to your weapon tip. This would be the sword hand and forearm. Think of it this way, if your opponent is attacking your chest, and you are attacking their wrist, you have less distance to go to place your blade, and you will hit first.

Again, think of your épée game as a duel. Be economical and efficient with your actions. Be logical. And definitely be conservative.

Sabre

The sabre is the third weapon of fencing and the last one you should study. It is most divergent from the other two, and, to get the most out of it, should therefore be approached with plenty of preparation (ie: foil and épée). This is my opinion; others do disagree with me. But I believe that slow and steady wins the race. If you decide to become a fencer, be in it for the long haul.

The sabre is of military origins, especially cavalry, although the modern version we use is definitely a streamlined version of the original, which was rather broad and heavy. It was molded into its present form to allow for a quicker, more maneuverable fencing game.

Sabre fencing resembles foil in that it is a conventional weapon (that is, with rules that govern the way it is used). But the resemblance ends there. With sabre both the point and the cutting edge of the blade may be used to deliver a touch. Unlike the foil and épée, which demand small, precise actions delivered from the fingers, the sabre employs broad, sometimes sweeping moves. The sabre is obviously the flashiest of the three weapons of fencing.

In sabre, the target area is everything from the waist upward, including the arms and head. In the ideal sabre

Sabre fencing

game, cuts and thrusts may be combined into complex exchanges, making it perhaps the most challenging weapon in fencing. For that reason alone, it should, as I've cautioned, be taken up only after studying foil and épée first. This will give you the strongest foundation possible for mastering the complexities of sabre play.

On Guard

The on guard position for sabre differs from foil and épée in that the sword hand is held toward the direction of the outside line, this to protect the outside of the sword arm from attack. Also, the free arm is held behind the fencer, hand on hip, to keep it from falling into the line of attack.

Sabre Lines

Sabre lines are different than those of foil and épée. Since sabre is fought entirely in pronation, we do not deal at all with supinated positions. Prime (one) covers your low inside line; seconde (two), the low outside line; tierce (three), the high outside line; quarte (four), the high inside line; and quinte (five), the head.

Holding the sabre

Offense

Sabre offense requires following rules of right-of-way, like foil. Attacks are made by both cutting and thrusting.

Cuts come from the forearm and fingers working in conjunction: as the sword arm extends, the blade is snapped forward from the fingers. This creates light but firm touches. Never make cuts from the shoulder. These will be too heavy and wide. Inefficient, wild attacks will always leave you open to counterattacks. Thrusts are made with a completely straight sword arm.

Defense

Cultivate your defense. Too many sabre fencers today just run at one another in a game of *fast draw* (trying to hit before the other fencer hits). In the Middle Ages, they called it *jousting*. Learn to hold your ground, parry and riposte.

Because the sabre deals primarily with cuts — which come in at all angles with a flexible whipping intensity – you'll find your defensive responses will generally require wider actions than either foil or epee. Small, pre-

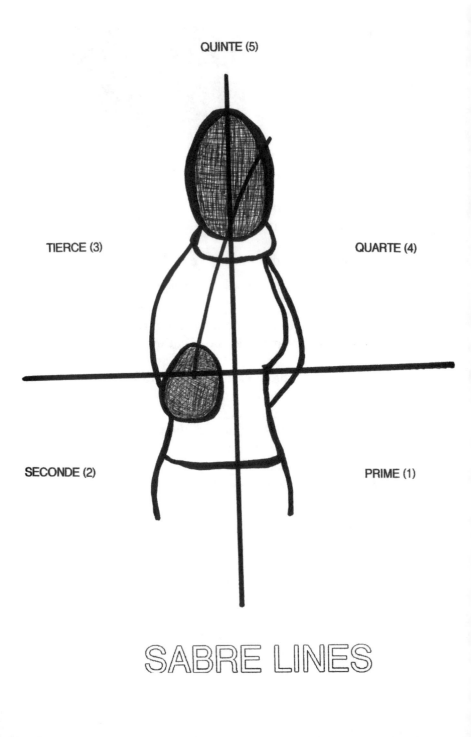

QUINTE (5)

TIERCE (3)

QUARTE (4)

SECONDE (2)

PRIME (1)

SABRE LINES

cise parries would never stop an opposing sabre blade as it cuts toward its target. This is a reality of the weapon.

Strategy

As I've already mentioned, sabre is a game employing both cuts and thrusts. This, of course, is traditional sabre fencing. Today, you will find countless sabre fencers who know nothing about point work.

I believe, therefore, that the best sabre strategy is to learn to integrate both cuts and thrusts effectively. Think how this will work against the sabre fencer who knows nothing about defending against the point. The fencer who masters this technique comes a formidable foe.

Also, balance your offense and defense. Never fall into the aforementioned *fast draw* mentality. Fencers locked up in this type of game are one note fencers and always leave themselves open to the parry riposte. Use this fact.

Don't make your sabre game a power play. Use your brain. Your fencing will only be as smart or as dumb as you make it.

Think!

FENCING TERMS

ADVANCE: Moving forward on the fencing strip.

ANGULATION: An exaggerated angling of the blade and sword arm at your opponent when attempting to maneuver around a defensive position.

APPEL: A stamp of the front foot.

ATTACK ON THE BLADE: An offensive blade maneuver used to overpower and deflect an opponent's blade before attempting to make a touch.

ASSAULT: A friendly fencing encounter.

BALESTRA: An attack comprising a slight forward jump followed by a lunge.

BEAT: Knocking your opponent's blade away offensively.

BIB (BAVETTE): Neck protection on a fencing mask.

BODY EVASION: An attempt to avoid an incoming attack by moving out of its way rather than by parrying.

BOUT: A fencing encounter where touches are counted.

BUTTON: The flattened tip of a sword blade.

CORPS A CORPS (body to body): A situation in which two fencers have come extremely close to one another, touching or nearly touching.

COQUILLE (shell): The hand guard on a sword.

COUNTERATTACK: Attacking against an attack.

CROISÉ: A parry and riposte made in a single flowing motion. It blocks an attack, diverting it with leverage, and hits without letting go of the blade.

CUT: Advancing the cutting edge of your blade at your opponent offensively.

CUTTING WEAPON: A sword designed to strike with its blade's edge.

DEROBEMENT: An evasive slide off an opponent's blade into the opposite line. Such a move may be performed against either an offensive or defensive action.

DIRECT ATTACK: An attack made in the same line in which the on-guard stance is taken.

DISARM: The act of relieving an opponent of his sword.

DISPLACEMENT OF TARGET: A situation where a fencer covers a valid target area with an invalid target area to escape being hit.

DISTANCE: The space between you and your opponent. Also called measure.

DRY FENCING: Fencing with standard, as opposed to electric, weapons.

ENGAGEMENT: Where two opposing blades are touching.

EXTENDED INTENSION ATTACK: An attack made whereby the intent to hit is not placed in the first offensive action executed but in a following one.

FALSE ATTACK: A full attack made without intent to hit. It may be done to test an opponent's defense or to draw a parry-riposte action that might be exploited.

FLANK (flanc): The portion of the torso immediately beneath the sword arm.

FLECHE (arrow): A forward leaping delivery of an attack.

FLICK: A forceful, sometimes brutal, offensive whipping of the blade.

FOIBLE: The weak portion of a sword blade.

FORTE: The strong portion of a sword blade.

INDIRECT ATTACK: An attack that deviates from the original line of the on-guard position.

INVITATION: An action designed to provoke a desired offensive response from an opponent so that it may be taken advantage of.

LAMÉ: The electric fencing vest.

LIEMENT (bind): An offensive action employing leverage that both envelopes and guides your opponent's blade out of line in a single smooth motion.

MAESTRO/MAITRE: A fencing master.

MAL PARRY: A parry that does not sufficiently divert an incoming blade away from your target area to keep it from touching.

OFF-TARGET TOUCH: Blade contact on a portion of the body that is considered invalid.

ON-TARGET TOUCH: A touch on an opponent's body in an area deemed valid.

PASS: Crossing one foot in front of the other while advancing toward your opponent.

PASSÉ: Blade contact that slides, without any direct point contact.

PETITE COUSSIN (little cushion): The padding on the underside of the sword hand guard.

PISTE: The fencing strip.

PLAQUÉ: Hitting flat with the blade without direct point contact.

POIGNÉE (grip): The sword handle.

POINT WEAPON: A sword designed for thrusting only.

POMMEL (little apple): The counterweight metal nut on the end of the sword hilt.

PREPARATION: An action or actions used to set up or facilitate an attack.

RASSEMBLEMENT: Bringing the feet together.

RECOVERY: Returning to the on-guard position after a lunge.

REDOUBLEMENT: A continuation of an attack in the opposite line after being parried.

REMISE: A continuation of an attack in the same line after being parried.

RETREAT: Moving away from your opponent on the fencing strip.

REPRISE: A continuation of an attack after a lunge when no parry has been made.

SCORING BOX: The electrical machine used to record touches in modern fencing tournaments.

STOP THRUST: Extending your blade into an opponent's attack without first parrying.

TANG: The portion of a sword blade that fits through the handle of a sword.

THRUST: Extending the point of your weapon toward your opponent offensively.

TIME THRUST: A blade extension made against an opponent's attack (without first parrying) that both blocks an attack and delivers a touch at the same time.

TIMING: The tempo by which an action, offensive or defensive, is executed.

TOUCH (touché): The valid hitting of one's opponent.

SECTION FIVE
BIOGRAPHIES

THE HELENE MAYER MYSTERY

The Nature of Excellence

It was the biggest sports extravaganza of all time: Hitler's Berlin "Nazi" Olympics of 1936. The Germans were determined to show the world that they were indeed the *master race* in every way. In spending 30 million dollars on their Olympics, it was easy to see that they would spare no expense to prove this.

The year 1936 was a volatile time for international sports. Because of its racist policies, Germany threatened to exclude Jews from competing on its team. Jews in various countries asked for a boycott of the games. The United States very nearly withdrew its team from competition. An alternative Olympics was scheduled to take place in Barcelona, Spain, but was cancelled when the Spanish Civil War erupted. The situation was charged and unsettled.

Into this turmoil stepped a tall, willowy blonde, a sports figure of international stature. Her name was Helene Mayer. She was an acclaimed fencer, a champion in a sport dominated historically by men. She was a German and she was most definitely a Jew.

Born in Offenbach, Germany, in 1910 of a Jewish father and a Christian mother, Helene demonstrated a flair for fencing at an early age. At 13, she became the women's fencing champion of Germany. At 17, she easily captured a gold medal at the 1928 Olympics in Amsterdam, Hol-

Helene Mayer's solid lunge

land, winning 18 bouts and losing just two. A year later, she became the women's fencing champion of Europe, then the equivalent of today's world championships. She repeated this feat again in 1931.

It has been said that Helene Mayer was the best woman fencer who ever lived. In fact, she probably could have beaten all but a handful of males fencers during her lengthy career. Trained in the classical Italo-German school, she possessed a strong desire for excellence. She not only won, but she looked good while she was doing it. She was a champion's champion.

Still, Helene Mayer was a Jewish woman in a country where Jews were held in disfavor. Helene felt the change in her homeland to such a degree that following her participation in the 1932 Los Angeles Olympics, she chose to stay in the United States, ostensibly to go to school at Scripps College in Claremont, California. She later taught German at Mills College in Oakland near San Francisco.

In 1933, in a swell of anti-Semitic fervor sweeping through Germany, Helene was publically written off the rolls of her home fencing salle, the Offenbach Fencing Club. To remain in the United States had proven to be a wise decision.

The 1936 Olympics, however, called out, and Helene was pulled back into the fire. And here questions arise.

A fencer of Helene's caliber couldn't just be discarded like so much trash. She was an international star. What kind of Olympics would it be if the very best didn't participate? But would Germany exclude a Jewish Helene from its team?

We find two stories existing from this time period. One says that the United States government pressured the Hitler regime into allowing Helene to fence for the good of amateur athletics. She couldn't, under existing rules, fence for any other country, such as the United States. If Helene didn't compete for Germany, she couldn't fence at all. The other story has it that Germany, not wishing to let the best woman fencer in the world slip through its fingers, wanted her badly. In their quest for world superiority, it is said they even rationalized away her Jewish heritage, explaining that because she had two "pure" German grandparents, the other side of her family, the Jewish side, was cancelled out.

Beneath this were rumors of threats against Helene's family if she didn't cooperate with the Third Reich. Of course, as history has shown us, Germany was not beyond strong-arm tactics.

But did Helene need to be coerced? To some today, it seems unlikely that she would have been eager to compete for a country that had openly vilified her. As early as 1934, the U.S. Olympic Committee thought it necessary to send her a number of letters urging her to attend the Berlin games. This seems to show a reluctance on

Helene's part to go. On the other hand, in 1935 she is-
sued a statement to the press announcing that she would
be pleased to represent Germany again internationally.
She even told Jewish groups who were calling for her to
shun the event to mind their own business. Was this the
action of a sportswoman who merely wanted to do what
she did best, regardless of the politics? Was she convinced
to fence for the sake of amateur athletics by the USOC?
Or, perhaps, was she putting up a front to ensure the
safety of her family back within the borders of Germany?

Doubtlessly, the story would be more easily decipher-
able if Helene's true feelings about her Jewish background were better understood. For instance, how much
did it influence her decisions? When asked, she always
referred to her racial origin simply as "German." And
there were her blunt remarks to the Jewish organizations
calling for an Olympic boycott. Yet, in 1932, she felt her
ancestry enough to remain in the United States rather
than return to an anti-Semitic homeland.

When the Olympics came, did Helene actually believe
that Germany's official view had somehow changed with
regard to her? In spite of Nazi hate campaigns against
Jews, people at large in her country continued to think
highly of her. Helene Mayer figurines sold well in Berlin
shops during the Olympics.

There doesn't seem to be any one strong point of view
here on which to base any clearcut conclusions. Was
Helene Mayer a victim? A collaborator? A hero? Or
merely a self-absorbed athlete? No one can say for sure.

It was into this world of complex contradictions that
Helene Mayer found herself a cause celebre. Whether
she wished to be or not, when the Berlin Olympics got
underway, she was a star.

The fencing tournament held at the 1936 Olympics
had 300 contestants from 31 nations. No other sport had
such a turnout. The competition was held in two gymnasiums and an amphitheatre and eight additional strips
had to be laid down on nearby tennis courts to accom-

modate the overflow.

The elimination process went on for a full two weeks. Fencers competed from morning to night. Endurance became one of the chief virtues of the competitors.

In the women's fencing (foil was the only weapon open to women at the time), a series of elimination bouts left eight fencers, three of whom are considered the best swordswomen of modern times.

Helene Mayer was never far from the limelight. Her bouts with Hungarian Ilona Schacherer-Elek (the 1934 and 1935 European Champion) and Austrian Ellen Preis (the 1932 Olympic Champion) were two of the most keenly watched contests in the 1936 Olympic games. Track-and-field events, of course, drew more press because that has always been the bread-and-butter of the summer games. And black running star Jesse Owens versus Germany was the stuff of headlines. But among aficionados of the Olympics, among the old-timers, fencing was the queen of the events, something to be followed with bated breath. Baron Pierre de Coubertin of France, the founder of the modern Olympic Games, was himself an avid fencer.

The hard-fought bouts between Helene and Schacherer-Elek ended up with the Hungarian slightly ahead. But, as the finals progressed, Helene managed to pick up points faster than her rival. Eventually, they were tied for first place.

It was Helene Mayer's encounters with Preis, however, that received the most attention. It has been said that their final bout together was "the most dramatic fencing match of the age." The atmosphere of this last contest was so tense that those watching the battle were almost too choked up to make any sounds. Amazingly, Helene and Preis ended up in a draw.

At the conclusion of the tournament, the three women were so evenly matched, indicators — touches received versus touches delivered — decided the victor.

When the dust cleared, Ilona Schacherer-Elek was the

Helene Mayer (left) at the 1936 Olympics

winner. Ellen Preis was third. Helene Mayer took second place.

And now for another piece of this complex puzzle.

While accepting her silver medal, Helene Mayer delighted the German audience by giving a perfect "Heil Hitler" salute. Was this nothing more than a gesture of a patriotic athlete, or was it an action of someone who'd been told how to behave by the Nazi propaganda machine? It does seem out of character for anyone with even the slightest Jewish background to have acted in this manner.

Suddenly, if we carry the confusion a step further, even Helene's taking second place becomes suspect. Was she fencing her best game for the Nazis, or was she holding back slightly, just enough to keep from winning handily? Curiously, the following year, she fenced in the 1937 World Championships in Paris, France, and walked all over everyone she faced, including Ilona Schacherer-Elek, the 1936 Olympic champion. Was her performance in 1937 an indication of what should have happened in 1936? Or did her 1936 loss simply spur her on to a strong win in 1937? More questions!

All that can be said with any certainty is that after her 1937 victory, Helene never fenced internationally again.

Helene Mayer returned to the United States, where she eventually became a citizen. While no longer participating in world tournaments, she still fenced in U.S. Nationals until 1947, when she retired from the competition trail altogether.

Helene now fenced purely for the love of fencing. She maintained her interest by helping young fencers at a school in San Francisco run by an old friend, Hans Halberstadt.

In 1951, Helene was forced to give up her sport entirely when she was diagnosed as having breast cancer.

What were the actual motivations that led Helene Mayer to the Nazi Olympics? Patriotism? Compulsive desire? Blackmail? When asked about the subject, she would never say.

In the final analysis, her story becomes a sort of *Citizen Kane*-type mystery, a story without answers, only questions. Some saw her as a great sports figure; others as a traitor to her heritage. The truth was lost forever with Helene Mayer when she died of cancer in Frankfort, West Germany, in 1953.

CHAMPION OF CHAMPIONS

Ilona Elek is considered by many fencing historians to be the greatest woman fencer of all-time. Others argue that the German fencer Helene Mayer was the stronger competitor of the two. Examining their careers side by side, it is safe to say, if nothing else, Elek was certainly Mayer's equal.

Born in Hungary in 1907, Ilona Elek achieved numerous victories in fencing over the years. She is, in fact, the only woman to win two gold fencing medals at the Olympics, in 1936 and 1948.

During the 1936 Berlin Games, she beat out the aforementioned Helene Mayer for the top position. When she won her next Olympic gold medal in 1948, at the Games in London, England, she did so with decisive wins over most of her opponents. Two dramatic bouts with Maria Cerra of the United States and Karen Lachmann of Denmark were her only truly difficult moments. Considering the fact that she hadn't participated in an Olympic competition in 12 years, and that she was at the time 41 years old, this was considered perhaps her most memorable accomplishment as a fencer.

But Elek's victories don't end there. She also proved her abilities in fencing's world championships. She won the world title in women's foil in 1934, 1935, and 1951.

Slightly lesser, but still important performances include: second place in the World's Championship in 1937 and 1954, and a third place in 1955.

Ilona Elek (center) at the 1936 Berlin Olympics

In 1952, at the age of 45, Elek appeared to be on the verge of winning her third Olympic gold medal. Indeed, she won her first 20 bouts in a row. But she tired towards the end of the tournament, losing her final three encounters. She still took the silver medal, however.

During the span of her long fencing career, Elek won more international fencing titles than any other woman. Certainly few fencers, before or since, have matched her outstanding abilities on the fencing strip. She was truly a champion of champions.

Ilona Elek died in 1988, at the age of 81.

THE ORGANIZER

Without Julia Jones Pugliese, the reality of modern women's fencing might be much different than what it now is. In a time when women, as a group, were looked upon as second class fencers, she interjected a voice that was both intelligent and firm, providing an impetus for positive change in a game that has often resisted new ideas.

Pugliese began her fencing career in the 1920s at New York University, under the supervision of the famed Spanish master Julio Castello. She immediately proved herself an adept pupil. Between 1929 and 1931, with the help of her coach, she became a formidable contender in the intercollegiate world, winning a number of championships.

Like many before her, Julia could have been content with her medals and simply moved on in life, just another woman fencer. But she envisioned a greater role for women in fencing than the one that had been allotted. Women needed and deserved a more positive voice in the game they were obviously contributing to.

In 1929, her passion for women's fencing led her to become a co-founder of the *Intercollegiate Women's Fencing Association* (IWFA). No more following in lock step, mute and compliant with decisions made by men alone. Women could be leaders, guiding their own fencing destiny. While the IWFA began with only four member clubs,

Julia Jones Pugliese

today, as the oldest sport-oriented women's intercollegiate group in the United States, its boasts dozens of member schools.

After college, Julia became a fencing coach, first at NYU and later at Hunter College. Years later, she became the first woman coach of a U.S. Olympic fencing squad. In her time as a teacher, she helped shape a number of top women champions.

After a long and productive life in fencing, Julia Jones Pugliese died in 1993 at the age of 84.

MEMORABLE AND INSPIRING

Among other things, Helena Mroczkowska Dow was a four time U.S. national women's foil champion and an Olympian. She was also a member of the only mother-father-son Olympic fencing trio in the history of the Olympics. In her time as a fencer, she was noted both for her superb footwork and her remarkable endurance on the fencing strip.

Born in 1917, Helena Dow took up fencing at Hofstra University and soon began a winning trend that she was to continue for her entire competitive career.

In 1939, she was the Intercollegiate Women's Fencing Association foil champion. She also led her school to the 1939 team title. During her senior year in college, she won her first Amateur Fencers League of America's (AFLA) Women's Foil Championship. This was in 1940. Later, as a top member of the New York Fencers Club, she kept up her winning ways as the AFLA's top woman foilist for 1943, 1947, and 1948. Her 1948 win included a memorable defeat of the nearly unstoppable Helene Mayer in a match that has since been described as truly inspired.

On four other occasions, Dow took either second or third in national competitions. Moreover, she was a member of four national championship fencing teams.

On a local level, Dow also won the New York Metropolitan Foil Championship six times during the 1940s. Today, medals for this event are awarded in her name.

Helena Mroczkowska Dow

Helena Dow's participation in the Olympics came in 1948, at the games in London, England. Although she won no medals, she nevertheless fenced with her customary style and grace. She retired from the competitive life soon after this.

Unable to turn her back on fencing, she returned to the game in the 1960s, eventually becoming the coach of Fairleigh Dickinson University's Rutherford campus women's varsity team from 1967 to 1969.

In 1980, she was elected to the prestigious Helms Hall of Fame.

As an unusual side note, Helena Dow's husband, Warren, and her son, Richard, were also members of U.S. Olympic fencing teams, the former in 1936 and 1948, and the latter in 1972.

Her teachers included Aldo Nadi, Rene Pinchart, and her own husband.

It has been observed that, besides being one of fencing's competitive luminaries, she was further considered one of its most generous personalities, providing room and board at her own house over the years for fencers who found themselves down on their luck or who simply needed a place to stay for a couple days.

Helena Dow died in New York, April 22, 1998, after a bout with cancer. She was definitely one of America's most memorable fencers.

THE PREMIERE
WOMAN FENCER

Janice Romary has long been considered the most outstanding woman fencer the United States has ever produced. As Janice Lee York, she began her fencing training with the great master Ralph Faulkner at Falcon Studios in Hollywood, California, and she was a winner almost from the very start. A natural talent on the fencing
strip, she captured numerous local and regional titles.

Later deciding to expand her training experience, she
worked under the expert fencing hands of both Aldo
Nadi and Giorgio Santelli.

In her lengthy fencing career, Jan Romary won more
U.S. national foil titles than any other woman fencer, a
total of 10 (1950, 1951, 1956, 1957, 1960, 1961, 1964, 1965,
1966, and 1968). She was also a member of 6 Olympic
fencing teams (1948, 1952, 1956, 1960, 1964, and 1968),
twice finishing in fourth place (1952 and 1956). This is
by far the best performance of any U.S. woman fencer in
the Olympics to date.

In 1968, at Mexico City, Romary was given the honor
of being the first woman to carry the U.S. flag into the
opening ceremonies of an Olympic Game. For the Los
Angeles Olympics, sixteen years later, she became the
first woman commissioner of fencing (she even performed in a short fencing exhibition with her old master
Ralph Faulkner, who was 92 years old at the time).

Jan Romary will most certainly be remembered as America's premiere woman fencer, a title she richly deserves. Few women have even come close to equaling her outstanding achievements, and perhaps, no one will ever surpass her sustained level of excellence.

Janice Romary

THE OLD LADY OF
USA FENCING

Elaine Cheris is living proof that fencing isn't just for the young. Her fencing career, which began at the age of 29, has spanned nearly three decades, and has produced numerous championships and honors.

Cheris came to fencing in a rather roundabout way. As the assistant athletic director for a Jewish community center in New Haven, Connecticut, she put together a fencing program. Deciding to take a few lessons to see what fencing was like, she immediately developed a taste for the game; and after only three lessons placed third in her first tournament. After six lessons, she was seriously considering training for the Olympics.

Normally, 29 is a bit old to start setting one's sights on major international competition, but Cheris approached her goal with a single-minded intensity. In 1979, she quit her job and began training full-time for the 1980 Olympic tryouts.

She had to overcome a certain amount of prejudice because of her age. Her first coach, the great black fencing master Uriah Jones, told her, "You will never be accepted. You won't be popular. Anything gets in your way, ignore it. You're too old; I'm black." She followed this advice — and continues to follow it — to the letter.

Elaine did indeed make the 1980 U.S. Olympic team, only to find the entire U.S. Olympic team boycotting the

Moscow games for political reasons. Still, she was on her way in big time fencing.

Since then, Cheris has been a competing member of three other Olympic teams: 1984, 1988, and 1996. At the 2000 Olympics in Sydney, Australia, at the age of 54, she participated as an alternate, barely missing out making the team by a single touch.

Other high points in her fencing career include being a member of the gold medal women's foil team at the 1987 Pan American games and a member of the gold medal women's épée team at the 1991 Pan American Games.

At the World Championships, she has been the member of numerous U.S. teams in both foil and épée. As for U.S. National Championship competitions, she has consistently placed highly over the years. At the World Maccabiah Games, in Israel, she was an individual silver medalist and a member of the gold medal team in 1981.

In 1983, Cheris was inducted into the Colorado Sports Hall of Fame. In 1993, she was awarded the Federation Internationale d'Escrime's Gold Medal of Honor.

She currently operates her own fencing club, *The Cheyenne Fencing Society* in Denver, Colorado.

Cheris remarks that people are always asking her why she doesn't just retire and leave fencing to the youngsters. Her answer: "Maybe I am too old to be doing this, but it is so much fun. ...It's something I want to do; I have a passion, so I keep doing it."

Elaine Cheris may be somewhat older than your average competing fencer today, but she is a long way from being over the hill. She is already looking toward competing in the 2004 Olympics in Athens, Greece. But regardless of future achievements or the opinions of those who do not appreciate the value of competitive courage, she is already an inspiration to young and old fencers alike.

Elaine Cheris

AFTERWORD

Another Side of the Sword

Unlike many of the women about whom you've been reading, I am not a champion fencer. I teach fencing at Westside Fencing Center in Los Angeles, California, and in my work there have been privileged to know and work with some of the finest fencers in the world, both men and women. My particular expertise with bladed weapons, however, differs slightly from theirs and from the heroines of this book: I am a choreographer, what Hollywood calls a swordmaster. As such, I work more with historical swords than with modern fencing weapons, and most of the people I train need to develop a set of instincts completely contrary to those of competitive fencers. For these reasons, the sport fencing classes I teach (as opposed to theatrical fencing) are in basic technique, which is common to both, and these students move on to learn their competitive skills from one of Westside's many world-renowned coaches.

You may ask, then, why have I been asked to contribute to this book. I admit, it was only by asking myself the same question that I discovered what it is that I have to offer a reader of a book on fencing for women. You have read tales of championship performances in these pages and perhaps been inspired by their accomplishments. We might recall such legendary fencing pioneers as Janice Romary (who still holds the foil championship

Roberta Brown

record for both sexes), Dr. Adelaide Baylis (our first national women's foil champion), and Mrs. Stuyvesant Fish (president of the Amateur Fencers League of America's — now the United States Fencing Association — first women's committee in 1929) — all women with whom I have become aware of through my work creating the Westside Fencing Center's internet website. No doubt we all assume that any athlete who reaches a top level of recognition, such as these women have done, has to overcome tremendous obstacles. There are, however, obstacles for women in fencing, as in many fields, which are unique to our genre. And these gender-specific obstacles I have found to be common to both sword choreography and competitive fencing.

Although we know historically that women have wielded swords for centuries, the examples we have are more exceptions than rules. One thinks of Joan of Arc, perhaps of the Celts, perhaps even of those two dueling semi-clad French noblewomen who have been the subjects of various woodcuts and paintings. More traditionally, however, when we picture an encounter involving swords, we picture men.

Ironically, I write this afterword from southern Spain, where I am on location shooting a television series called *The Queen of Swords*, in which I double the heroine for all of her sword fights. This has been a learning experience in many ways, including one that strikes me as particularly pertinent to this book. I discovered on the first day of shooting that a very probable reason why so few women were renowned for their accomplishments with the blade in centuries gone by is that physical activity in a tight corset leads to discomfort so extreme as to be virtually prohibitive! While the men with whom I invariably engage in battle wear clothes that encourage movement, the women's costumes, which are more or less specific to the period of Spanish colonial California, bruise me with every move. I say this not as a complaint against either the costume designers or society in general, but rather as an observation about societal expectations: Women in most cultures have not historically been expected to engage in physically aggressive activity, and our clothes, until relatively recently, have reflected societal expectations. With this in mind, it is interesting to note that Joan of Arc dressed like a man and our two French noblewomen removed their more restrictive garments.

I do not mean to imply that clothing has stopped women from excelling in fencing. This book is clear testimony to the contrary. However, restrictive clothing is an obstacle that women have had to deal with in competitive fencing as well. Of the many challenges a male fencer faces on the strip, high heel shoes and skirts do not figure into them. We have photographic evidence, however, of women so attired from as early as the late nineteenth century — most notably, perhaps, being the wonderful troupe of Viennese fencers who toured the U.S. in 1888, giving many people their first glimpse of women skilled at swordplay. These photographs, along with other images of early fencing pioneers such as the early twentieth century Yale Women's Fencing Team and even a 1933 *New York Post* cover of a woman fencer, all depict the athletes dressed in skirts and heels, to say nothing of the no doubt incommodious period undergarments. In fact, it was Joanna de Tuscan, the remarkable sabre fencer so dramatically ahead of her time, who first fenced a bout at the 1935 Nationals wearing trousers, causing an unprecedented stir in the New York press. One response came in the form of an article entitled, "Pants are for Guys," by Paul Gallico, in the April 25, 1935, *New York Daily News*. In addition to taking issue with Ms. de Tuscan's attire, he also observes, "A lot of the girls kept their hair very messy, or it got messy while they fenced ... I don't see why a gal can't fix to be athletic and dainty at the same time, too ..."

The trouser event did seem to have a lasting effect on the fencing rules, however, as the next rule book put out by the AFLA, in 1937, specifies that after September 1, 1939, women may wear either what is referred to as a "divided skirt" or "loose-fitting white trousers fastened below the knee." (Interestingly, the divided skirt option for women remained in the rules well into the 1990's, although after the 1960s no one seems to have taken advantage of it.) Other gender specific fencing rules have included the regulated separation of male and female fencers, fewer touches per bout for women, the exclusion of women from fencing with certain weapons, the exclusion of women from full membership of the AFLA for many years, and, interestingly, the exclusion of certain female body parts as target areas. Specifically, even though male foil fencers were allowed to target the groin area from 1923 onward, female fencers were asked to mark a visible line on their jackets — running across their hip bones — to clearly delineate the illegal target area which lay below — until 1960.

All of these rules and commentaries, in my opinion, reflect a societal tradition that, through the ages, has generally discouraged or even forbidden women to take up arms. Today, of course, these imbalances are a thing of the past, and fencing rules allow for an equal footing (though women fencing sabre is an issue still not entirely settled). What I have observed, however, is that centuries, and indeed millennia, of societal mandate are not so easily shaken off and that many modern women who now begin this sport still have some subliminal obstacles that men rarely face. Both among the actors I teach and among the hopeful fencers who take my beginners' fencing classes, I have observed that women in the 21st century, women who have grown up with more or less the same opportunities as men, are frequently still hesitant to throw themselves into what is, essentially, an aggressive activity.

I have been fortunate enough to teach either fencing or stage combat (theatrical fencing) in several countries, including England, the U.S., Colombia, Austria, and now Spain, and my observations of women students apply across the board, without regard to international boundaries. Although each of these cultures produces strong women in all fields, in every instance I have found that the majority of women I teach have a significant obstacle to overcome in embracing a physically aggressive activity. Moreover, most of these women, had you asked them beforehand, would not have imagined that they had such an obstacle.

As we begin a new millennium, most of us feel that we are unaffected by the antiquated limitations faced by our predecessors and that we are now free to fulfill our potential without regard to external notions of gender. However, in my teaching experience, 75% to 85% of the women I teach find some difficultly in attacking another person, and I think that this is the residue of countless years of both subliminal and clearly stated messages that to be a woman, to be feminine, to be all that a female should be, is not to behave aggressively. I am not disputing either way on the subject of what constitutes femininity, and the feminist soapbox is not my launching point. I simply offer the observation that the majority of my female fencing students invariably begin their fencing experience not wanting to hit me, and that their counterparts in the world of film and theatre generally hesitate to commit fully to an action which in fact only impersonates an attack.

When I studied and later taught stage combat in London, stage combat was required for male students, but many drama schools made it an optional class for female students. This, in my experience, perpetuated the attitude that swordplay was not an intrinsically feminine skill; and thus even the women who took the class generally had lower expectations of what they could accomplish than their male classmates did. The same attitude, really, is reflected in the fact that women to this day do not compete in the Olympics in sabre and have only relatively recently begun competing in épée, both of which are seen as more aggressive weapons than the foil.

What is perhaps unique in my perspective is that, because I teach a combination of beginners and actors, my students are not necessarily athletes (or at least not yet!), but as such it is possible that they are a more representative cross-section of society than the upper echelons of a fencing salle might be. Whatever the explanations, however, my observations of these beginners imply that many women are still hindered by invisible barriers left over from previous generations, and that these barriers have been overcome by the most successful women fencers.

My point is that a book on women in fencing is more than an obvious tribute to a group of athletes and champions who share a common gender. It is a tribute to a group of athletes who have had to overcome invisible obstacles unknown to other fencers and at times unknown even to themselves. It gratifies me to observe that at this time approximately one half of both my fencing and stage combat students are women, and I enjoy helping them acknowledge and overcome the hesitancies I have described. When a woman lunges with power and thrusts forcefully at my chest, when a woman swings a broadsword with ferocity and commitment, I get to share all over again in the exhilarating, freeing sensation I myself felt the first time I allowed myself to truly experience the power of wielding a weapon.

The world, as the cliché goes, is changing, and the women whom this book in part pays tribute have played a major role in changing popular attitudes toward how we move, how we express ourselves, and what we contribute to sport. As in many sports, these first women champions are the pioneers who make it possible for the athletes who follow them to picture themselves succeeding and standing on podiums with ribbons around their necks. Our clothing no longer restricts us, laws no longer restrict us, and even tradition has ceased to restrict us. As we succeed more and more, as these women have done in overcoming our own invisible obstacles, I believe we will continue to succeed dramatically in changing societal expectations and fulfilling our own.

For all of these reasons, I applaud the writing of this book, and I am honored to have been asked to participate in its creation. These pages cannot help but be filled with inspiration. I hope you have read them with this sense.

Roberta Brown
July 2000

APPENDICES

ORGANIZATIONS

Sport Fencing

THE UNITED STATES FENCING ASSOCIATION (USFA)
1 Olympic Plaza,
Colorado Springs, CO 80909
e-mail: info@USFencing.org
The guiding organization for sport fencing in the United States. Founded in 1892 (as the Amateur Fencers League of America), the USFA sponsors tournaments, guides the U.S. international fencing effort, and publishes a quarterly magazine (*American Fencing*).

Classical Fencing

THE ST. LOUIS CLASSICAL FENCING SOCIETY (CFS)
web address: http://www.nurble.com/kabal
The CFS trains fencers in the art and science of classical fencing and provides information regarding the classical fencing process. It also acts as a link between like-minded clubs and individuals.

IN FERRO VERITAS (IFV)
1045 Codington Road,
Ithaca, New York 14850
e-mail: info@classicalfencing.com

IFV provides training and information regarding classical fencing.

Historical Fencing

HISTORICAL ARMED COMBAT ASSOCIATION (HACA)

8746 Aberdeen Palms Dr.,
Houston, TX 77096
web address: http://www.thehaca.com

HACA promotes and explores western martial arts through workshops and independent study.

ASSOCIATION FOR HISTORICAL FENCING (AHF)

P.O. Box 2013,
Secaucus, NJ 07096
e-mail: jumbs@ahfi.org

The HFA provides training seminars, workshops, and lectures highlighting historical styles of combat.

Coaching

THE UNITED STATES FENCING COACHES ASSOCIATION (USFCA)

P.O. Box 274,
New York, NY 10159
e-mail: gregpaye@hotmail.com

The USFCA is an organization aimed at serving the United States fencing coach community. Their programs include: accrediting coaches, workshops, apprenticeships, and activities representing coaches' interests.

Theatrical Fencing

THE SOCIETY OF AMERICAN FIGHT DIRECTORS (SAFD)

1350 Flamingo Road, #25,
Las Vegas, NV 89119

SAFD is an organization for theatrical fight directors. They also sponsor major workshops for both fight directors and actors.

Role-Playing Combat

THE SOCIETY FOR CREATIVE ANACRONISM (SCA)
P.O. Box 360789
Milpitas, CA 95036
phone: (800) 789-7486

The SCA is a historical role-playing group with a strong emphasis on the Middle Ages and the Renaissance. Founded in the early 1970s, they have chapters all over the world. The SCA holds tournaments and fairs and publishes literature regarding their various interests.

SUGGESTED READING

The following is a recommended list of books that will improve your understanding of fencing:

AMBERGER, J. Christoph. *The Secret History of the Sword*. Burbank, California: MultiMedia Books, 1999.

BARBASETTI, Luigi. *The Art of Foil*. New York: Barnes and Noble, 1998. Reprinted from the 1932 edition.

BURTON, Sir Richard F. *The Book of the Sword*. New York: Dover Books, 1987. Reprinted from the 1884 edition.

CASTLE, Egerton. *Schools and Masters of Fence*. York, Pennsylvania: George Shumway, 1969. Reprinted from the 1885 edition.

DE BAZANCOURT, Baron Cesar. *Secrets of the Sword*. Bangor, Maine: Laureate Press, 1998. Reprinted from the 1900 edition.

EVANGELISTA, Nick. *The Art and Science of Fencing*. Indianapolis, Indiana: Masters Press, 1996.

EVANGELISTA, Nick. *The Encyclopedia of the Sword*. Westport, Connecticut: Greenwood Press, 1995.

EVANGELISTA, Nick. *The Inner Game of Fencing*. Chicago, Illinois: Contemporary Books/Masters Press, 2000.

GAUGLER, William. *The History of Fencing*. Bangor, Maine: Laureate Press, 1998.

GAUGLER, William. *The Science of Fencing*. Bangor,

Maine: Laureate Press, 1997.

HOBBS, William. *Fight Direction For Stage and Screen.* Portsmouth, New Hampshire: Heinemann, 1995.

LANE, Richard. *Swashbuckling.* New York: Limelight Editions, 1999.

MORTON, E.D. *Martini A-Z of Fencing.* London: Queen Anne Press, 1992.

NADI, Aldo. *The Living Sword.* Bangor, Maine: Laureate Press, 1995.

NADI, Aldo. *On Fencing.* Bangor, Maine: Laureate Press, 1995. Reprinted from the 1943 edition.

WESTBROOK, Peter, with Tej Hazarika. *Harnessing Anger: The Way of an American Fencer.* New York: Seven Stories Press, 1997.

WISE, Arthur. *The Art and History of Personal Combat.* Greenwich, Connecticut: Arma Press, 1971.

FENCING BOOKS BY WOMEN AUTHORS

The following is a list of fencing books written by women:

The Book of Fencing (1930), Eleanor Cass
Fencing (1966), by Muriel Bower and Torao Mori
Fencing (1969), Nancy Curry
Foil Around and Stay Fit (1977), Camille Lownds
The Fencing Book (1984), Nancy Curry
Foil Fencing (1996), Muriel Bower
On Guard (1997), Donna Jo Napoli
Fencing: Steps to Success (2000), Elaine Cheris

FENCING MAGAZINES

Today, there are basically two fencing-related magazines in America.

American Fencing Magazine
1 Olympic Plaza,
Colorado Springs, CO 80909

American Fencing Magazine is the in-house magazine for the United States Fencing Association, covering the progress of organized sport fencing in America.

Fencers Quarterly Magazine
6751 County Road 3850,
Peace Valley, MO 65788

Fencers Quarterly Magazine (formerly *Veteran Fencers Quarterly*) is an independent publication dealing with all aspects of fencing, from history, to philosophy, to technical, to personalities. Its slogan is, "Fencing gear for the brain." This magazine is published by the authors of *The Woman Fencer*. *FQM's* website is located at:
http://users.townsqr.com/ale/fqm.htm

CONTRIBUTORS

NICK EVANGELISTA

Nick Evangelista is a fencing master with over 30 years experience. His specialty is the classical French school of fencing. He has written four other fencing-related books: *The Encyclopedia of the Sword* (Greenwood Press, 1995), *The Art and Science of Fencing* (Masters Press, 1996), *Fighting with Sticks* (Loompanics Unlimited, 1998), *The Inner Game of Fencing* (Contemporary Books, 2000). He is also the editor-in-chief of *Fencers Quarterly Magazine*, and the fencing editor for *Encyclopedia Britannica*.

The former assistant of fencing master Ralph Faulkner, he now teaches fencing in Missouri. Nick Evangelista plans to never retire from fencing.

ANITA EVANGELISTA

Anita Evangelista has been fencing on and off for almost 28 years, and she likes épée much more than foil. Outside fencing, Anita is registered nurse (RN, BSN), an EMT, a hypnotist, and college student on her way toward a masters degree in psychology. She is also the author of a number of books on a variety of subjects: *Hypnotism: A Journey into the Mind* (Arco Books, 1980), *The Dictionary of Hypnotism* (Greenwood Press, 1991), *How to Develop a Low-Cost Family Food-Storage System*

(Loompanics Unlimited, 1995), *How to Live Without Electricity – And Like It* (Loompanics Unlimited, 1997), and *Backyard Meat Production* (Loompanics Unlimited,1997). She has also co-authored two books with Nick Evangelista: *Blood-Lust Chickens and Renegade Sheep* (Loompanics Unlimited, 1999), and *Country Living is Risky Business* (Loompanics Unlimited, 2000). She is the managing editor of *Fencers Quarterly Magazine*.

Anita is also a photographer and artist. Furthermore, she is listed in the prestigious *Who's Who in the Mid-West, Who's Who in America,* and *Who's Who in the World.* She has been Nick Evangelista's companion/wife for 27 years, and has two children (both now adults), one of whom fences.

POLLY CRAUS AUGUST

Polly Craus August is a former United States fencing champion (national women's foil championship: 1949) and a member of two U.S. Olympic fencing teams (1948 and 1952).

When she retired from fencing, she spent many years as an administrative assistant to fencing master great Ralph Faulkner. Outside the fencing world, she worked in the film industry as a production assistant. Polly is also a housewife and mother.

ROBERTA BROWN

Roberta Brown has taught theatrical fencing and swordplay at such places as Hollywood's *Howard Fine Acting Studio, The Lee Strasburg Institute,* Bogota Columbia's *Teatro Libre,* London's *Webber Douglas Academy of Dramatic Art, The University of Southern California,* and *The Westside Fencing Center,* where she also teaches sport fencing.

Her swordmaster, choreography, and coaching credits include dozens of theatrical productions, as well as film and TV projects.

In addition to teaching swordplay privately to some of Hollywood's high profile actors, she also teaches children's classes in Los Angeles schools.

Another major fencing project in which she takes great pride is the creation of the *Westside Fencing Center* website (www.westsidefencing.com), which features an ever-growing online fencing reference library.